Exploring
Costume History
1500-1900

VALERIE CUMMING

Batsford Academic and Educational Limited   London

C.55

First published 1981
© Valerie Cumming 1981
ISBN 0 7134 1829 X

Printed in Great Britain by
The Anchor Press Ltd
for the publishers
Batsford Academic and Educational Limited
4 Fitzhardinge Street, London W1H 0AH

Contents

Acknowledgment

I am indebted to many colleagues in museums, libraries, record offices and art colleges for their ideas and comments on project work, costume history, and other allied subjects, and I hope that they will forgive me for not naming them individually. Over a number of years I have evolved my own approach to project work for students of costume history, but I am immeasurably grateful to the authors whose excellent, specialised studies of various aspects of this subject have made the research for this introductory book such an enjoyable experience.

My particular thanks go to Stella Newton, who taught me costume history, and who suggested my name to Batsford as a potential author; to Kay Staniland, who shared her wide knowledge of the subject with me during the five years we worked together; and to Olivia Bland, for her helpful comments on the manuscript and excellent typing.

I am grateful to Thelma Nye, Belinda Baker and Clare Sunderland of Batsford for their assistance with the typescript and illustrations, and for making the production of my first book such an interesting experience.

Finally, I would like to thank my husband for his interest, patience and good humour throughout the period when this book dominated our lives to the exclusion of everything else.

List of Illustrations

All of the illustrations marked with an asterisk * are taken from generally available museum and art gallery publications eg postcards, catalogues and booklets.

COLOUR PLATES

BLACK AND WHITE ILLUSTRATIONS

Introduction

Costume history is an increasingly popular subject, as a component in examination syllabuses in schools and colleges, as an interesting option for term work, or as a subject for adult education programmes. This book was written for students who want to study costume history, but who need guidance in assessing the various sources and types of information which are generally available. Although the contents were compiled with the particular needs of secondary school students in mind, the methods which are outlined are also relevant to an older audience who want to find out more about costume history.

Each year large museums, libraries, record offices and many other specialised organisations receive numerous project letters. The basic content of these letters is usually: 'Please send me all the information and illustrations that you have on . . .' Most organisations have neither the time nor the number of staff to cope adequately with these enquiries, nor should they be expected to undertake this work. Projects are not set in order that students should crib all their information from these organisations and their hard pressed staff. They are set to provide students with a new and more sophisticated type of work which gives them opportunities for individual effort while investigating the sources of information which surround them.

Costume history is like a jigsaw puzzle with relevant pieces to be found within a number of disciplines, including social history, literature and the fine and applied arts. However, like all complex subjects it is based on a central core of knowledge, which must be adequately mastered before more ambitious work is undertaken. This book is concerned solely with this central core, the history of fashionable dress in England from 1500 to 1900. Nearly all garments worn in western society were either current fashions or, like legal dress, had been fixed by tradition. Exotic influences were introduced as novelties, but they only became popular when they were adapted to fit into the mainstream of contemporary fashion.

This book contains very little discussion of costume outside these limits, because it is liable to be misunderstood until the student is familiar with the major central changes of costume history.

It was decided to begin at 1500 because this is the starting date which is chosen by many examining boards for their students. This does not imply that costume can only be studied seriously after this date, but it does provide an appropriate, if arbitrary, starting point for students whose advanced studies in history or literature usually begin with the post 1485 modern period. The terminal date of 1900 was chosen to ensure that this book would be a manageable length. All the methods of study suggested in these pages are still applicable to the period after 1900 which can be approached through the many excellent recent publications which are available from bookshops and libraries.

How to use this book

The entire contents are planned to provide information on how to tackle project work. The first part, Chapters 1 – 3, explains how to discover what information is easily available, how to assess it before choosing a topic for a project, and then how to assemble and present the project. Part 2 outlines the various historical strands which can be woven together to create a rounded and effective piece of work. All of the information in Part 2 is intended to leave unanswered questions which students can follow up for themselves by referring to the books listed in the bibliography.

It is important to use all of the sections of a book. The bibliography which lists suggestions for further reading; the glossary which explains unusual or obsolete words; the list of illustrations and their sources, and the index which provides a shortcut to particular subjects, are all essential clues to unravelling the puzzle of where to find additional information. When a good deal of time is available for finding information it is always sensible to read all of a relevant book. However, when time is limited, or when a lot of the information looks familiar, intelligent shortcuts can be taken by making use of the ancillary sections of a book. An example is given on the following page.

Choice of Project: Men's Suits 1665-1700

1   Consult the *index* under Suits (Men's) and read the pages referred to, and look at the illustrations which are listed.

2   Make a note of any unusual words eg 'cassocke' and look for a definition in the *glossary*.

3   Refer to the *bibliography* for further reading, but look under all the possible headings, menswear, general histories of costume, seventeenth and eighteenth-century costume, cut and construction.

4   Acquire useful illustrations by referring to the *list of illustrations* and by writing to the relevant organisations (including a stamped, addressed envelope) for their publications list and order form.

There is no definitive method of study which suits everyone, and no book, however skilfully written, will ever replace individual effort when it comes to finding information, but by using the complete contents of this book intelligently, every student will be able to master the basic skills of project work.

Part 1
Project Work

1 Finding information

The arrangement of the chapters in this book is intended as one of the keys to a method of approaching a project. Too many students choose a subject for a project without considering how they are going to find the necessary information. Ideas for projects should always spring from a careful assessment of how easy or difficult it will be to compile information in the available time.

There are four main rules about finding information. The first is to study the written sources; the books and magazines which can be found in libraries. The second, which only applies to those who are confident about using original documents, is to look for additional, unpublished information in the local record office. The third stage is to see if it is possible to arrange a museum visit to look at surviving examples, armed with questions which the staff there may be able to answer. Lastly, but possibly the most important rule of all, students should try to make the best possible use of their local sources of information. Public libraries, record offices and museums are located throughout the country, and they exist to serve the needs of their local communities, so make good use of them. It is unwise to apply to large national libraries, record offices and museums in the first instance. They are so fully stretched that their facilities are really only suitable for experienced students who feel they have exhausted the possibilities of their local services.

In establishing contact with any of these services it is worth remembering that staff in all these organisations are busy people who will respond more readily to requests for help if the enquirer can show evidence of having made some efforts on his or her own behalf. If the nearest library or record office or museum is to be contacted in the first instance by letter, it is always a good idea to enclose a stamped, addressed envelope for the reply.

Libraries

Many schools and colleges have excellent libraries and they will acquire books on the various subjects which are studied by their students. However, if they do not have many books on costume, the next step is to go to a local library. In large towns or cities there will be books on costume in both the lending library and in the reference library. Small branch libraries, however, may have to borrow books from another branch, or from elsewhere in the country through the national inter-library loan service.

Libraries nearly always contain bibliographies on a wide variety of subjects. These short booklets contain lists of books, magazines and journals on specialised subjects which libraries stock or can obtain from elsewhere. The two most readily available bibliographies on costume are *A Reader's Guide to Costume* (Publication No.126) which is published by the Library Association; and *Costume, A General Bibliography* written by P Anthony and J Arnold, and published by the Costume Society. Many libraries also produce their own lists of books according to subject classification, or they will sometimes have a card index which lists books under subject headings.

There are books on other subjects which contain useful information for the student of costume history, namely books on textiles, embroidery, social history, art history; and biographies, memoirs and diaries. These may contain useful quotations or illustrations, or throw a sidelight onto the subject which a costume history book does not contain. It is useful to spend time in a library locating all the different sections that might produce helpful books. When pressed for time it is sensible to glance through the index of a book under any of several headings such as clothes/costume/dress/fashions to see how many relevant page references such a book contains. It is a good idea to carry a small pocket book in which potentially interesting books can be listed; this list can be invaluable when paying a visit to the library.

When books can only be found in the reference section of a library, it is often possible to cut short the time needed for taking notes by deciding which sections or pages are relevant and taking photocopies of them. Nearly all libraries contain photocopying machines with a slot payment system of between 5p and 10p per page. This facility is particularly useful when illustrations are difficult to acquire, as most machines are capable of reproducing them well if the original is a clear one.

Certain libraries with good local history sections will contain a great deal of interesting information on local trades, crafts and manufacturing industries, and it is always sensible to enquire about such a service. Such sections often hold old photographs or prints of the area, some of which might be reproduced for sale, others of which might be available for photocopying purposes. Many of these photographs or prints will show figures, and it is important to remember the need for, and the availability of illustrations when looking at information with a view to choosing a project theme.

Obviously there are a great many books which are not available from local libraries. Rare books or magazines, or some books published 50 or more years ago, can only be seen in specialised libraries. Such libraries are intended for the experienced student, and should not be approached until it is certain that the relevant books cannot be seen elsewhere. None of them are lending libraries, so time must be put aside for a visit to their study rooms. University libraries are only open to registered students, but in London it may be possible to use the library of the Victoria and Albert Museum or the British Library. For both of these it is necessary to apply for a ticket, and to be sponsored by a lecturer. To work in the British Library it is usually necessary to be over 21 and a postgraduate student. However, there are two important costume libraries in other parts of the country which will take students by appointment, namely the Fashion Research Centre in Bath, and the Gallery of English Costume in Manchester.

Record Offices

Record offices and libraries are mandatory public services, which means that all local authorities are required by Act of Parliament to provide them in their areas. However, unlike libraries, record offices have no lending function, and there is usually only one record office in each county. They exist as repositories for all records connected with the work of local authorities, and a great many private records. The latter category includes wills, inventories, records kept by local industries and businesses, and a variety of personal papers such as letters and diaries.

Some of the larger record offices have an education officer whose job it is to introduce schools and colleges to the various categories of records housed there, and to suggest ways in which students can use records when working on projects. The type of information which might interest the student of costume history can sometimes be found in wills, inventories and letters of particular individuals, or in the records of small local businesses or industries whose production or distribution of clothing or cloth took place in a particular area of the country. In Part 2 of this book there are references to the particular products of various areas of the British Isles, and depending on where a student lives, this could provide a suitable line of enquiry.

All record offices, even those without officers, have a 'search room'. This is the part of the record office which any member of the public can enter during opening hours with a request to see documents related to his or her particular interest. If a student is unsure about what records the local office contains, it would be wise to write or telephone to explain what sort of work is intended and whether records are an unfamiliar area of study. It is important to remember that many of the documents in record offices will be difficult to read. Until comparatively recently all documents were handwritten. Such handwriting may be difficult to decipher, or the abbreviations and construction of language may be obsolete and hard to follow, consequently reading records can be a very time-consuming business.

The attraction of working with records, or archives, as they are sometimes called, is that the documents may not have been used for a long time, and the student may have the opportunity of being the first person to present them to a reader in a new form. However, they will only contain part of the information that is required, and additional time will have to be spent seeing how this new evidence accords with published material of a similar date.

Some students may feel ready to try this sort of work, but if there is any uncertainty, it would probably be wiser to concentrate on published sources in books, magazines and journals.

Museums and Art galleries

Although museums are not a mandatory service there are many hundreds of them, both large and small, throughout the British Isles, Their major concern is with the collection, care and presentation of artefacts to the public. What can be seen in the galleries of a local museum is usually only a fraction of the collections, so even if there is no costume or related material on display, it is likely that there may be some in the reserve collections. In the *ABC Guide to Museums and Art Galleries,* which is published annually, and which can be consulted in a reference library, there is a long list of museums arranged by county. Each short entry mentions the type of material which the particular museum collects. There are over 120 museums and galleries which collect costume. In Janet Arnold's *Handbook of Costume,* which is available from many local libraries, there is a detailed list of about

70 costume collections throughout the British Isles.

It is a curious fact that students constantly send enquiries to the large costume museums in London, Bath, Manchester, Edinburgh and Cardiff, but seem unaware of the facilities of their local museums, many of which have an education officer or a costume curator who might be able to help them. It is a tremendous temptation for many students to start with the museum, perhaps expecting that this will prove a short cut to answering the problems presented by a costume topic. However, nothing is more calculated to annoy a busy costume curator than a letter asking for information of the sort which can easily be found in a local library.

However, it is obviously a great advantage to a student to be able to look at surviving dresses, suits, accessories or whatever it is that interests them. Nothing is quite as exciting as seeing an original dress, looking at how it was made, studying the material and trimmings, and making notes and drawings. But to get the most out of a visit of this kind it is necessary to prepare by reading relevant books and looking at any public displays of costume, so that the limited time that a curator may be able to spare can be used intelligently.

Not all museums have the facilities or staff to cope with visits of this kind. Some museums have education services which offer specialised tuition to school parties and students in the form of group sessions or public lectures. These can be very rewarding, but if they are not detailed enough it would be sensible to enquire whether there is a costume curator who might be prepared to see groups of students or individuals who want to look at surviving items of costume and discuss particular problems. Do not expect too much from these visits. If they can be arranged, time will always be limited, and the numbers and types of item that can be seen will be restricted.

Many museums, apart from the well known ones, publish leaflets, catalogues and postcards which provide information about their collections. A new publication which deals specifically with this subject is *A Guide to Costume and Textile Publications from Museums in Great Britain*. It lists many of the museums which sell anything of this nature, and gives addresses for further information about availability and cost. Museum publications provide much more illustrated information on surviving items of costume than can be found in the average costume history book, for a comparatively small sum of money.

Apart from costume publications many museums offer other services which may be relevant for students. Museums should be visited regularly as both their displays and their publications change year by year. Displays on such subjects as textile machinery, embroidery or photographs can add an extra dimension to the study of costume. If the shortage of publications on a particular subject is a disappointment to a student, he or she should take the opportunity of writing a polite letter to the museum, saying how enjoyable and instructive the displays are, but how useful a small publication would have been. The knowledge of public demand for such items strengthens a curator's case when he has to argue for money to invest in publications.

Art galleries can often provide a wide range of illustrations which are suitable for costume history projects. English painting has always been dominated by portraiture, and many galleries contain dated portraits of a wide variety of sitters. There may also be paintings of groups of people; these are a valuable guide to the various forms of dress that were worn at a particular date. Unless a student has been studying costume for a number of years it is unwise to consider undated paintings, and caution should also be exercised over paintings which contain figures whose dress seems unlike other examples of the same period. The figures could be dressed in theatre costume, fancy dress or ceremonial dress, or the type of timeless draperies in which certain late seventeenth- and eighteenth-century painters preferred to dress their sitters.

2 Choosing a project

Once a student has become familiar with the sources of information which are available, the choice of project may still be difficult to make. Possibly the local facilities are excellent, and consequently the choice of topics may seem limitless. This is the stage at which it is probably wise to take advice from a tutor or local museum curator. What can be undertaken is, of course, limited by several factors: firstly the amount of available time in which the work has to be researched and written, secondly the number of words which are required, and thirdly whether the choice is limited by an examination syllabus.

There are two main traps into which a great many students fall at this stage if they fail to take advice, or have no-one who is able to advise them well. The first trap is the 'blanket coverage' topic. This may well spring from a worry that 2000–5000 words is an immense number to write and therefore it is easier to write at length if a long period is chosen. Museum curators are familiar with confident letters stating that the enquirer is intending to write about 'the history of wedding dresses' or 'women's fashions from 1400 to the present day'. If this type of subject is set by an examination board there is obviously no escape, and a method of coping with this will be outlined later. However, if the topic is a matter of individual choice, it is wiser to choose a short period because this allows space to discuss the developments which effected changes in costume. Long periods usually result in simple lists of changes in fashion which are difficult to write and exceedingly boring to read. Very few students have to write projects which are more than 5000 words in length; many only have to write between 1000 and 3000 words. This sounds a great deal; in fact it is hardly the length of an average newspaper article. Each of the chapters in Part 2 of this book is just over 2500 words long, and these are the briefest introductions to the major themes in each of the periods under discussion. It is always worth considering that if an author can write a 60 000 word book on eighteenth-century costume, 1000 words on the same subject will seem hopelessly superficial.

The second part of this book is divided into periods ranging in length from 50 years to 100 years. The information given in each of these chapters provides starting points from which all kinds of themes and topics can be explored in greater depth.

The amount of information on costume which is readily available to the average student is not infinite, but it is considerable, and much more enjoyment and satisfaction can be gained from examining a short period in detail, rather than by skating over the surface of several centuries.

The second trap is that of the specialised topic. This is usually combined with the blanket coverage approach, and is equally doomed to failure. It may seem original and imaginative to choose a project on theatre costume or ceremonial dress, or on the history of umbrellas, buttons or knitting, but finding books which deal specifically with these topics is a difficult task. There may be occasional references to all of these subjects in other costume books, but putting the information together may well prove to be the equivalent of doing a jig-saw puzzle when many of the most vital pieces are missing.

Costume history is like every other subject in that the structure of knowledge must be built on sound foundations. This book is concerned with these foundations. There are a great many ideas which can be explored at this level of knowledge, without worrying about the more sophisticated topics which even an experienced costume historian might find difficult to complete successfully. The current preoccupation with clothing for specific occasions: weddings, periods of mourning, sports, or clothing for particular occupations: farmers, servants, workers, lawyers; or the study of associated accessories: umbrellas, shoes, fans and gloves, is fine if the foundations of knowledge have been built soundly, but these subjects are full of pit-falls for the beginner.

Naturally there are parts of the country where the local industry was umbrella making or button manufacture. The local museum may devote a large display to the subject, the local reference library may be full of old newspaper cuttings about the factories and craftsmen, and the record office may contain fascinating trade books, but this is certainly not the case throughout most of the country. This is an instance of how intelligent students can afford to follow their own inclinations. Local trades and manufactures can and should be investigated if there is enough evidence to support such investigation, and preliminary enquiries about local sources of information will lead naturally towards a particular topic which may yield interesting discoveries. Nearly all areas in the British Isles produced cloth or accessories at some stage in history, but it is essential to find out whether the relevant information is easily accessible before deciding to embark on specialised topics.

Students who live in an area still renowned for its wool cloth or its cotton materials may be so used to this knowledge that they long to escape into an unknown area of costume history. This is perfectly understandable, but it is also a sad waste of the resources available to them. Wool and cotton are the two most important textile-manufacturing industries in the history of this country. Studying their development in relationship to the changing fashions and the demand for them will provide the most rewarding results.

Many students have particular talents or interests which lead them quite naturally towards a certain type of project. Others are fortunate in that their teaching staff or examination syllabuses contain set topics which have been carefully selected to suit a wide range of abilities. For both categories of student the methods of work which are outlined in this book, and the information found throughout it, are still applicable, but can be adopted to suit their individual requirements. For those students who are uncertain about making a choice there is a section on suggested projects towards the end of this book. These are divided into categories, and labelled according to the ease or difficulty the student may experience in completing them successfully.

Some examination boards are less flexible and set only one topic. Presumably this makes marking easier, but it can be disheartening for the student who for one reason or another may find the topic uninteresting. One such topic, set in a recent syllabus, was 'Collars and necklines from Tudor times to the twentieth century', and a 1000 word text was required. The premise behind this choice of topic was presumably that it covered the whole period required by the syllabus, but was less difficult to cover if one aspect of dress was highlighted. In reality, such a topic probably produced a mild sensation of panic in all the students who realised that this covered 495 years, which allowed just two words of description for each year.

Obviously such a topic is no real test of the students' knowledge or abilities, it is just a test of their mechanical skill in being able to précis large chunks of information. However, while such topics continue to be set it is no help to tell a student that he or she is attempting the impossible. Some method of work has to be recommended which squeezes some interest out of such an unpromising subject. In this instance students need to equip themselves with three or four well illustrated general costume histories, and divide up the period into centuries. The illustrations are the major clue to this sort of exercise, preferably those which show men and women together. Ten or twelve illustrations (postcards, photocopies, or drawings) of major changes in fashion can save a great deal of writing, so that the text of the project can concentrate on answering the questions posed by the changes. Taking, as an example, the ruffs and standing collars which were worn in England for much of the sixteenth century up until the 1620s, the questions which ought to be answered would be:

How did they start?
When were they at their largest?
Were they the same for men and women?
What were they made of?
How were they decorated?

These questions will be answered in the various costume books, and by looking at the illustrations the students will be able to add their own observations. If there is enough space to write something about their cost, how they were made, whether they were worn by all classes in society, and whether they were a purely English fashion, this will make the project more interesting.

The outline approach, given above, can be applied to many types of project. It is more rewarding when the period is a shorter one, simply because there will be more space for discussion of the various aspects which enliven a topic, effectively removing it from a catalogue of year by year changes. When dealing with a long period, the pleasure of finding, sifting and arranging information into an interesting and attractive presentation is prevented by the pressure of fitting as much detail as possible into the requisite length.

Attitudes towards costume history have altered considerably in recent years, and the student searching for a topic may be uncertain about the sort of subject matter or information which is required. Several of the examination boards which provide syllabuses have very definite views about the breadth of knowledge they expect a student to acquire. Apart from a familiarity with construction they often mention understanding of the technical advances in the clothing industry; the effect of social and economic change on fashion; the influence of literary and artistic movements; the role of designers, and the means by which fashion is popularised through magazines, films and television. This sounds formidable, but any student with an enquiring mind will find a good deal of this information en route to compiling a project.

Opinions about costume vary wildly, from a

belief in the importance of being able accurately to reconstruct garments, through a spectrum of shifting emphases on the clothing worn in a certain period or in a particular context, to the sociological and psychological interpretation of the significance of clothing. The last category is the most treacherous one for the inexperienced student as it encompasses many attractive but spurious theories about costume. Certain basic premises about the role of costume as a means of communicating ideas of social aspiration, or of official position, or as a means of coping with a particular form of work or leisure can be grasped fairly easily, and can enrich a project, but the complicated theories are best left for the sociologists and psychologists to argue over.

The one indisputable fact about costume is that its effect is primarily a visual one. This is not to ignore the effect it will sometimes exert on our other senses, but the initial impression is always of appearances. Illustrations are the key to the understanding of dress in all its forms, or surviving examples if any are available. Initial curiosity is always aroused in this way, and the other investigative processes follow on naturally from this point. If students want to find inspiration for a project, it can develop naturally if they allow themselves time to assimilate a strong visual awareness of the subject. Just leafing through books on painting or photography, or looking at statues or monumental brasses can trigger off an insatiable curiosity to know more than the visual evidence can tell the viewer.

If this chapter appears to counsel caution at the expense of originality, this need not be a dampener on creative energy. The choice of a project is of paramount importance, and the best results will always be attained by students who are prepared to reserve their decision until they have investigated the feasibility of what they want to do. Caution does not rule out choice, but it does prevent worries and disappointments.

3 Presenting a project

The presentation of a project is most important. Finding relevant information and attractive illustrations is two-thirds of the work, the final third is the use of this material and its arrangement on paper. An intelligent and attractive presentation of the information for a project is additional evidence of interest in, and understanding of, the subject matter.

Nearly all projects either form part of an examination syllabus, or are submitted as part of a term's work. In both instances certain guidelines will be set down by the school, college or examination board. They will specify the length of the project, the number of illustrations which should be included, and whether the finished text should be handwritten or typed. Such guidelines should always be respected. No examiner wants to read 3000 words written in illegible handwriting and carelessly interspersed with drawings and pictures, if the guidelines asked for 5000 words of double spaced typing with all the illustrations placed as a central section in the piece of work. Marks for presentation can make all the difference between a pass and a fail mark, or between a good pass and a distinction.

Good presentation stems from logical methods of work. There are ways of collecting information and arranging it, so that the final effort of writing and presentation is a logical conclusion to all the previous hard work, and not a frantic race against time. Chapter 2 mentioned a simple outline method of collecting information in answer to particular questions, and Part 2 of this book demonstrates a method of arranging notes on a particular period according to specific headings.

These section headings are only a sample of what might be appropriate. Individual students may wish to work with fewer headings, or with more, according to the needs of their own projects. The wisdom of using this method is that it enables the student to assess quickly what type of information is lacking. It does not mean that the finished project should necessarily be divided up in this manner; various categories of information can be interwoven or kept separate as the student wishes. Each heading may only require one sheet of paper if it is a short 1000 word project, or several sheets if it has to be a longer piece of work.

Once a topic has been selected for a costume

history project it is important to think of both written information and illustrations as part of an integral whole. Illustrations should be acquired and selected alongside written notes, with the intention of using both as methods of presenting information.

Note taking is a time consuming business, and it is sensible to read a book first, or the relevant sections of it, think about how relevant its contents are to the topic, and then write the notes under the various section headings. Contemporary quotations can enliven a piece of work, and many of the publications recommended in the reading list at the end of this book will provide this type of material. It is, of course, more rewarding for students to find their own quotations, from plays, novels, letters, but there may not be the time to do this sort of additional reading. Again this is an area in which the student who is working with local sources may be able to make interesting new discoveries in a local reference library or record office.

The format for the project may depend on the guidelines mentioned earlier or be left to the student. A short piece of work may be easier to write as an extended essay with a few sub-headings, but a longer piece of work will certainly benefit from being divided into sections or chapters. These sections will almost certainly develop naturally from the type of information the student has been able to find, but if there is any doubt about this aspect of the work, it would be sensible to discuss the matter with a teacher or tutor before starting to write.

A possible format for a 3000—5000 word project on 'Women's Costume 1750-1790' might be:

Brief introduction
Outerwear, describing the construction and
    changes in these fashions, including materials
Underwear, briefly mentioning stays, hoops,
    chemises, petticoats
Accessories
Dressmakers, including other types of shopping,
    and the likely costs
Conclusion
Glossary
Book List

The value of an introduction is that it can be used as a place in which the scope of the project is discussed. If the student wants to concentrate only on wealthy and fashionable women, the introduction is the place where this can be stated, so the examiner is not under the impression that she is marking a project which will attempt to discuss all women's clothes in that period. The inclusion of a glossary and a book list will make the most simple project seem more professional. A glossary is not essential,

although it can prove a useful method of coping with obsolete words without breaking up the main text of the project with explanations.

The layout of the text of the project should be neat and spacious. One difficulty which all writers on costume history face is that of making the subject of clothes sound interesting. Inexperienced students may find this difficulty almost insurmountable, so they should be especially careful that what they do manage to write is in clear, logical English, well punctuated, and without spelling mistakes. Each page of the text should be numbered, and the completed piece of work should be firmly held together in whatever manner the school or college prefers — in a folder, or stapled together or held with tags through punch-holes.

The illustrations are a matter of individual choice, and each student will decide how he or she wishes to illustrate their projects. The most obvious types of illustrations are postcards, pictures cut out from magazines or colour supplements before they are disposed of, drawings, photocopies, diagrams and photographs. Postcards can be obtained from a wide variety of sources; museums, art galleries, stately homes, specialist card shops, and rarely cost more than 5p or 10p each. At the beginning of any project it is sensible to write to the publications officer of museums, enclosing a stamped, addressed envelope, asking for a copy of their publications leaflet. From this it is possible to see what is available that might be relevant to a particular topic. Many students often have opportunities to visit museums as part of their curriculum, and over a period of time it is possible to build up a useful file of postcards on a variety of interesting subjects. Some museums produce leaflets or catalogues on costume which are well illustrated, and these can be cut up, or photocopied or traced for inclusion in a project. Photocopies, like postcards, are relatively cheap. The only disadvantage is that the majority of them do not reproduce colours, but this is a minor problem.

Students who are confident about their abilities to make detailed and accurate drawings will find this an invaluable skill. Apart from drawings taken from books, or paintings in galleries, or sculpture and brasses in churches, it is useful to include drawings of original items from museum displays or items which have been seen on visits to a local museum's costume department. These drawings should include notes on the distinctive features or the method of construction, and the type of material and its colours.

Although photography is so simple today, it is not always easy to get permission to take photographs in museums or stately homes. Even when such permission can be obtained the results may be disappointing because of low lighting levels or because the objects are behind glass. Some museums offer a photographic service whereby small black and white prints of some items in their collections can be ordered. However, this is not always a speedy process, and it can be fairly expensive, so it is sensible to make enquiries about whether such a service is available and what the likely cost will be.

Collecting illustrations for a project can be a frustrating business, particularly if a student tries to find this type of material at the last moment. This is why it is so important to assemble all the material together, and not leave everything until a few weeks before the project should be finished. Illustrations which have been carefully selected can save lengthy explanations in the text, and enhance the impact of the written word. For this reason their arrangement is just as important as the neat layout of the text. It is important to ensure that all illustrations are neatly trimmed, although variations in size are not important, and to place them in the same sequence as the ideas in the text to which they are related.

Illustrations always require captions, but these can be brief. They should draw attention to the features which are central to the theme of the project. If the materials, or the accessories or the construction of the garment is what the reader should look at, this should be stated in the caption. If the illustration is a copy of a coloured original it would be sensible to mention this. It is a good idea to state the source of the illustration, so that the teacher or tutor can check them if they are dubious about this aspect of a project. These sources can be quoted beneath the illustration, or in a complete list which is placed at the beginning of the project.

Where the illustrations should be placed in the text may have been decided by the examining board. If this decision is left to the student it need not cause concern as there are only two main methods in which they can be placed. The first method is to put them all together in one large or several smaller groups; the second method is to place them throughout the text, as closely situated as possible to the points which they illustrate. Whichever method is chosen it is sensible to keep them physically apart from the pages of the text. The weight of postcards, drawings etc. and the heaviness of a strong glue will buckle and distort writing paper. All illustrations should, if possible, be stuck onto sugar paper or cartridge paper. The advantage of this type of paper is that both sides can be used without causing any distortion. The illustrations should be numbered, so that this number can be inserted in the text to draw the reader's attention to the relevant picture and caption.

Drawing together the various strands of information into an attractive and intelligent presentation is rather like doing a jig-saw puzzle. At the outset it may seem difficult or confusing, but once all the pieces, in this instance the notes and illustrations, are laid out on a table, it will soon be possible to see how they can be fitted together into a coherent whole. Unlike the classical play or a novel, a project does not necessarily have a beginning, a middle and an end, but it can be helpful to think of it in that way. The beginning is the brief introduction to the subject with an explanation of the scope and approach which has been chosen; the middle will present the information according to this approach; the end will draw together any conclusions that may occur as the project unfolds. It is likely that until the first two sections have been written no conclusion will have presented itself. However, on re-reading the first two sections it is likely that a number of ideas will crystallise into a conclusion. Conclusions do not need to be original theories (these are rare in all subjects) but observations of any noticeable recurring devices or styles.

Good presentation will not disguise indifferent work, but when it is allied to thoughtful and reasoned analysis of the assembled information, the project will be a pleasure to read, and an achievement which can be regarded with considerable satisfaction.

Part 2
The Historical Background

1500-1599 Tudor Grandeur

Dress in all its forms is an expression of individual taste within the limitations imposed by the status, occupation and financial circumstances of its wearers. In sixteenth-century England fashions changed comparatively slowly, and at any one date a variety of styles were being worn. Young wealthy courtiers who wanted to make a good impression adopted new fashions more readily than older, less wealthy folk. However, by studying the major changes of fashion it can be determined how quickly such changes were accepted or modified by the majority of the population.

Although there are few books which deal specifically with sixteenth-century costume, useful information can be found in the many social histories and biographies which discuss the leading personalities and social changes of Tudor society. These books explain the growing prosperity and self confidence of the English nation at home and abroad. This confidence found expression in the bulky, swaggering and highly decorated clothing of the period (1). Many luxury goods were imported, and with them a variety of French, Spanish, Dutch and Italian fashions which the English people assimilated without losing their own strong sense of identity. England was fortunate in having its own thriving export trade in wool cloth, which provided many types and qualities of cloth to satisfy the home market and the foreign merchants.

Although sixteenth-century costume looks uncomfortable and impractical it provided layers of attractive but sturdy insulation in the badly heated and draughty houses of the period, and it was possible to conduct business, to travel, ride and hunt with comparative ease when dressed in these clothes.

Menswear

The garments worn by men at the beginning of the sixteenth century continued in one form or another to dominate their dress until the second half of the seventeenth century. From the body outwards these consisted of a shirt, a doublet, hose, a jacket or jerkin worn over the doublet, a gown or later in the century a cape or cloak. These garments came in a variety of shapes and combinations throughout the century. It was not necessary to wear all the garments at the same time; a particular occasion or the climate usually dictated the number of items which were worn.

DOUBLET

This was a closely fitting garment, usually padded, with long sleeves. The neckline was a low square or oval line revealing a good deal of the shirt until the mid 1530s, when it was more usually closed up to the lower neck, developing a collar after about 1540. The collars increased in height until the 1570s, and were then reduced to allow room for a ruff to be worn. The doublet might have a skirt. These are particularly evident in the 1530s and 1540s when they were longer and fuller as a balance to the wide shoulders and fuller sleeves of the doublet and gown (1).

1 Henry VIII with Henry VII, cartoon by Hans Holbein 1536-37. Henry VIII's broad shouldered gown, full skirted doublet and wide toed shoes contrast sharply with the narrow lines of Henry VII's long, loose fitting gown of 30 years earlier

When all this heavy fullness subsided, the doublet took on a new line, developing a pointed waistline with only the shortest of skirts or tabs. From the mid 1570s the body of the doublet was distorted by the addition of extra padding above the waistline. The contemporary name for this shape was a 'peascod belly' and it copied a Dutch fashion (2). As the doublet became shorter and less exaggerated the

2 **Sir Francis Drake by an unknown artist c.1585. Fashionable menswear of the late Elizabethan period included a 'peascod belly' doublet, with pinked sleeves, knee-length breeches, a short cape, a double row lace ruff and overshoes**

sleeves narrowed, developing puffs on the upper arm in the 1570s, and then the whole sleeve curved and widened from the later 1570s onwards.

Early in the century doublets sometimes fastened to one side, but front fastening, using buttons, laces and some hooks and eyes was the usual method from the 1530s (*4*). Decoration was an important element in a century when the silhouette changed fairly slowly, and popular variations were the slashing or pinking of the cloth (*colour plate 1, facing page 24*); the application of braids and embroidery or the use of extra features such as hanging or detachable sleeves (*5*).

JACKETS AND JERKINS

These were similar in line to the doublet, but with a longer skirt. They were usually worn open and caught at the waistline. In their many forms they might be sleeved or sleeveless. Leather jerkins, made of buff (dressed ox-hide) were popular between the 1540s and 1570s.

HOSE

This was an all purpose word which covered both breeches and stockings, which were, in fact, sewn together until the 1570s. They were close-fitting, rather like tights, although from *c*.1515 the upper section was fuller and made from a different material. Between about 1540 and 1570 these upper sections became oval in shape as a forerunner of the later trunk hose (*4*). The crutch was emphasised by a cod-piece, a fashion which survived until the 1590s (*1*). This was a flap fastening tied with points, and it was usually padded and decorated with embroidery.

After 1550 there were two main types of hose: trunk hose and breeches. The former were round, padded garments which were never longer than mid-thigh length, and from about 1570 they were worn with canions, which were knee-length, fitted extensions sewn to the trunk hose, but usually made of a different material. Breeches became fashionable in the 1570s and could be either full-bodied or close-fitting, but they were always knee-length (*2*). The hose and doublet were tied together with points, which were laces or ribbons with metal tips rather like boot laces.

OUTERWEAR

Gowns were fashionable with young men until the 1570s when they were displaced by cloaks (*3*). They were loose-fitting garments with

3 Brass of William Cobb Smythe and his wife Alys 1522. Brasses often show rather conservative fashions, as they were frequently executed during the lifetime of their subjects; both husband and wife are wearing the narrow gowns of the early sixteenth century.

23

4   Sir Nicholas Throckmorton by an unknown artist *c*.1562. Menswear was at its most elegant in the early Elizabethan period; the doublet and trunk hose were fairly narrow in line; caps and gloves were plain and the neck frill and cuffs were a modest size.

a fitted yoke, a rolled collar, wide shoulders and an open front. Ankle-length versions were popular with older men, or as informal garments rather in the style of dressing gowns. This type of long gown is the ancestor of the various ceremonial gowns worn in a number of professions up to the present day.

Cloaks were fashionable from 1545 onwards (*4*). They were three-quarter circles in construction and came in three lengths: to the waist, the thigh or the ankle.

UNDERWEAR AND INFORMAL DRESS

Shirts were the only form of underwear worn by men in the sixteenth century. These were made from widths of linen in a simple T shape, but often beautifully embroidered with black or coloured silks or edged with cutwork lace. The neckline of the shirt grew higher as the doublet collar developed and extended, but the body and sleeves remained unchanged. Nightshirts were longer versions of the shirt. Nightcaps were embroidered caps worn on informal occasions, but not in bed. A quilted waistcoat was often worn under the doublet, but never by itself except on very informal occasions.

Colour plate

1   Earl of Leicester by an unknown artist 1575-80. The Elizabethan delight in decoration is shown by the braids and pinking on the doublet, paned trunk-hose, the fur lining of the gown, the frilled ruff and cuffs, the jewelled buttons and formal chain

24

2

3

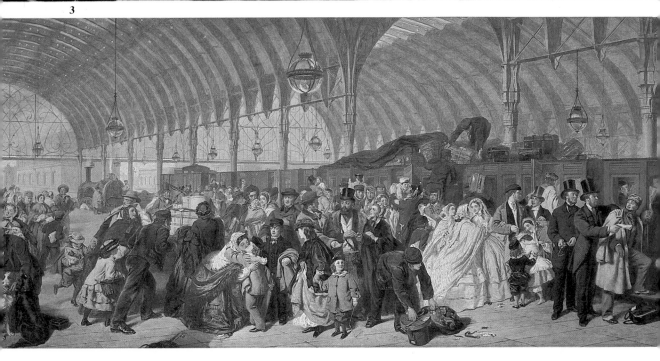

ACCESSORIES

The most noticeable items among the many accessories which men wore or carried in the sixteenth century were their headwear, their neckwear and their footwear. Caps and bonnets were the usual head-wear until hats started to appear in the 1570s. Until that date they were flat rather featureless items, made of a variety of materials from the knitted caps of apprentices to the velvet ones of richer men (1). Small, stiffly-blocked hats, worn at a jaunty angle, became fashionable in the 1570s.

Footwear altered with the fashions, the flat, wide fronted shoes of the period c.1510-1540, echoing the wide bulky garments (1), gradually developed a narrower line with a rounded toe, and, by the end of the century, a narrow wedge heel had been introduced. Overshoes were worn to protect the soft leather shoes (2), but boots, until the last years of the century, were only worn for riding or travelling.

Although a good deal of shirt front was seen in the early years of the century (1), it was only after 1540 that the neckband of the shirt became the 'falling band' as it turned over the doublet collar. Ruffs developed from the frilled upper edge of the shirt, becoming an important feature in the 1560s (4) and a separate item by about 1570. At first they were single, goffered bands, but additional layers were added in the 1580s requiring supports to keep them in place (5).

Women's clothes

When looking at the fashions worn by women, although the outside show may appear graceful or distorted, discreet or over-decorated, the distinctive shape of the garments owed everything to the structural undergarments, the corsets (or bodies, as they were called in the sixteenth century) and skirt supports. These always provide the key to how a particular line or style was achieved.

GOWN AND KIRTLE

The gown was a one piece overdress with a fitted bodice and a full skirt falling into soft folds which was often looped up to show its lining (3). The neckline was a low square which revealed the smock edge and part of the kirtle bodice; the sleeves of the gown were waist-length, either narrow or funnel-shaped. The kirtle consisted of a bodice and skirt, sewn or tied together with points. After the mid 1540s when the two sections were separate items, the name kirtle referred only to the skirt.

The gown was often worn over the kirtle until the 1530s, when it became relegated to the status of an optional over-gown. The kirtle had a bodice with a low square neckline which was stiffened with whalebone, and acted as both a dress bodice and a corset. From the later 1520s the sleeves were full and bell-shaped with a deep turn-back cuff, with contrasting undersleeves held at the shoulder by buttons or points. The undersleeves sometimes matched an underskirt.

The line of women's clothes changed quite slowly in the sixteenth century, from the narrow, graceful silhouette of the early years of the century, to a triangular shaped skirt matched by fuller sleeves in the 1520s. This shape, with changes in neckline and sleeve widths, retained its hold until the 1570s. These variations closely matched those occurring in menswear over the same period. The wide skirts were supported by a farthingale, a Spanish fashion which appeared

Colour plate

2 **Lord Capel and his family by C Johnson c.1639. Adults and children, with the exception of the youngest, were identically dressed; the looser, high waisted doublets and wide lace trimmed collars are mirrored by the female garments; rich glowing, plain satins were a feature of dress from the 1620s**

Colour plate

3 **The Railway Station by W P Frith 1863. The sober, sensible appearance of the men in dark suits and practical overcoats is in striking contrast to the light coloured, wide skirted dresses, loose shawls and fussy accessories of the women**

5 Queen Elizabeth I, engraving by C van der Passe *c*.1588. The elongated bodice and wheel farthingale distorted the natural figure; the impracticality of this style of dress is emphasised by the prodigal use of decoration, the long hanging sleeves and the large half ruff

early in the century, but gained popularity after the 1540s. In the 1580s wheel-shaped farthingales began to be worn (*5*), alternating in favour with the less cumbersome 'bum-rolls'. The fashionable silhouette in the 1580s and 1590s was very exaggerated, the bodice lengthened, the skirt extended into a full circle, the sleeves widened and the neckline was emphasised by large ruffs and standing collars.

Women's gowns were fastened at the front by ties or clasps, but bodices were usually laced at the back.

OUTERWEAR

Fur-lined gowns were popular in the second half of the century; but for travelling or riding, cloaks and safeguards (an extra skirt) were worn for extra warmth and protection.

UNDERWEAR AND INFORMAL DRESS

The female equivalent of the shirt was a smock, made in the same way and similarly decorated. Over the smock was worn a skirt support and the stiffened 'bodies', then a number of silk or linen petticoats. For informal occasions linen embroidered jackets and loose robes were popular.

ACCESSORIES

The key to the seemingly endless types of accessories, and the many styles of headwear, neckwear or footwear which were worn at the same time, is the sixteenth-century admiration for decoration. Clothes were patterned and trimmed, but extra indivduality was added in the form of soft leather goods, jewellery, lace and feathers. This must be viewed within the context of slowly changing styles, when small novelties were valued more highly because they signified change and individual taste.

English materials

WOOL

English wool cloth was a major national product in the sixteenth century. It was available in various weights, types and colours, and played a valuable role in the export trade to Europe. Nearly every part of the country produced enough wool to fulfil local needs, although the resulting cloths were not always of the best quality or in such varied types as were available from the main centres. The areas of large scale production were the West Country, East Anglia and West Yorkshire. Broad cloths came from the west, worsteds from the east and the cheaper narrow cloths from the north.

In the 1560s, under the patronage of Queen Elizabeth I, refugees from the religious persecutions in the Low Countries were allowed to settle in East Anglia where they used their weaving skills to produce wool cloths from much finer yarn. These clothes were lighter and softer, and draped well, and they were known as the 'New Draperies'.

LINEN

From the beginning of the sixteenth century until the middle of the eighteenth century a series of Acts of Parliament were passed in an attempt to encourage the English linen industry. These provided bounties for flax growers and import duties on foreign linens, but production was never extensive, and much of the yarn came from Ireland or Scotland, so linen remained an expensive material.

COTTON

At the end of the century small quantities of cotton were imported from the near East, and the production of fustian, a cotton and linen mixed material used for linings and cheaper types of clothing, was established in the area around Bolton by immigrant weavers from the Low Countries.

Foreign materials

SILK

This was the most expensive and luxurious material available to courtiers and other wealthy members of English society. All the categories of material which were woven from silk: velvet, damasks, brocades, satins, were imported from Spain and Italy. The designs on patterned silks were not specially woven for particular markets; it is possible to see similar materials worn by sitters in portraits throughout Europe. The silks for embroidering were also imported.

LINEN

The finest quality linen, and some coarser grades, were imported mainly from the Low Countries and from Germany. The former was a major production and trading centre for linen throughout this period.

LACE

Italian lace was one of the most highly prized forms of trimming. During the reign of Mary I ruffles made from lace 'commonly called cutworks' were forbidden to anyone whose status was lower than that of a baron.

Makers and construction

All formal items of clothing worn by both men and women were made by tailors. Tailoring was a long established and highly skilled craft, and its practitioners were carefully monitored by the powerful tailors' guilds. During his long training a young apprentice learned how to measure a customer and assess his or her special needs, how to cut economically from the expensive materials, and how to sew and trim a garment which would satisfy a customer's expectations.

Tailors were knowledgeable about changing fashions, materials and trimmings, and guarded their patterns, from which all garments were adapted to suit individual customers, very carefully.

The cutting out and sewing of linen undergarments and items of informal wear like jackets, caps, coifs, was the responsibility of the female members of a family, although the grandest households might employ sewing women to do this work. The simple lines of these garments did not tax their ingenuity, but the fine sewing and embroidery that they worked is often of a very high standard. Patterns for these garments and embroidery designs were adapted from existing garments, although by the end of the century many more designs were available in the form of pattern books.

Shops

All items of clothing, with the exception of certain accessories, had to be made up to a customer's individual requirements. This involved a number of purchases, visits to mercers and haberdashers to choose materials and trimmings and then consultations with the tailor about the style of the garment which was required.

Traders in certain goods tended to congregate in particular areas of a town or city. In London, for example, mercers and haberdashers had their shops on London Bridge. These shops were usually single rooms on the ground floor of a house, with workrooms and living accommodation in the same building. Clothes were expensive, but they were seen as an investment, and garments were often repaired, retrimmed and turned, before being disposed of. Courtiers who needed a great many clothes often sold their unwanted garments through secondhand clothes dealers in order to recoup some money before ordering new garments.

The standards of tailors and other craftsmen were vigorously monitored by their own guilds. In 1524 John House, a Norwich tailor, was fined 'for default of workmanship of a kirtle and a petticoat'.

There were few shops outside the larger towns and cities, but journeymen tailors, embroiderers and pattern drawers travelled throughout the country to customers who needed their services. There were also regular fairs, at which materials, trimmings and accessories could be purchased, and 'chap-men' or 'cheap-jacks' travelled widely carrying a range of small goods to remote areas.

Prices

These are only a small sample of the widely varying prices that could be paid for goods:

1522   For a woman's gown — 11 yards of tawny satin, £4 11s 8d, 2½ yards of tawny velvet, 33s 4d, a roll of buckram , 2s 8d, stuffing cloth for the pleats 11d and for making it up, 5s

1523   For a black velvet woman's bonnet, 15s

c.**1550**   For the gold thread and embroiderer's work on a doublet, jerkin and hose for Edward VI, £28

1555   For a doublet — 2 yards of holmes fustian, 20d

1568   For a red satin damask kirtle with a train, 20s

1569   For a pair of white leather pumps, 14d

1576   For one dozen yellow silk points, 6d

1581   For 5 yards of baize, 12s 5d

1586   For 6 yards of ruff lawn with cutwork and gold lace 60s

1591   For a black gown faced with budge and lined with lamb, £5 10s

Technical developments

No advances were made in the area of yarn production and its subsequent weaving into cloth. All the carding and spinning of yarn was done by hand, and the cloth was woven on the draw frame loom, a late fourteenth-century invention.

KNITTING

Hand knitting was introduced into England in the sixteenth century as an attempt to stem the flow of knitted goods imported from France, Italy and the Low Countries. These goods included caps, gloves, stockings and small items of clothing, and by the 1580s many of them were being produced in England.

In 1589 William Lee, a clergyman from the Midlands, invented a frame for knitting stockings which would do the work of several hand-knitters. However, he received little support for this new invention, and he eventually settled in France where he secured the patronage of Henry IV.

Surviving costume

No complete pieces of sixteenth-century costume have survived. What do survive, although not in any quantity, are knitted items, small pieces of embroidered costume and some accessories.

Knitted items, such as caps, and leather footwear have been recovered from archaeological excavations. Embroidered linen items such as shirts, gloves, coifs and nightcaps have probably survived as examples of fine sewing. Although a number of museums in this country may have one or two examples from the sixteenth century, perhaps an excavated shoe or cap, or an embroidered coif or night-cap, the collections which have the most comprehensive selection of items within this very limited range, are:

Victoria and Albert Museum, London

Museum of London

Museum of Costume, Bath

Gallery of English Costume, Manchester

As these items are rare and often very fragile they are not always on display, and usually cannot be handled by students.

1600-1659 Court and Commonwealth

One constant source of surprise to foreign visitors to England was how well all classes in society were dressed. Ragged peasants, of the European variety, were almost unheard of in England. Sometimes the fashionable aspirations of the lower classes actually led to the prohibition of certain types of material or garment. During James I's reign servant girls were forbidden to wear velvet and farthingales, and their ruffs were restricted 'to four yards in length before the gathering or setting of it'.

The growing group of religious dissenters, usually called the Puritans, disapproved wholeheartedly of fashionable frivolities. They considered that extravagant dress and luxurious accessories were a sign of the shallowness and corrupt values of the ruling social class, and should be condemned rather than copied. They dressed quietly and conservatively, avoiding all fashionable excesses. Their clothes were made of dark wool cloths, relieved by a small amount of white linen in the form of collars and cuffs. When the Puritans achieved political power under the Commonwealth, rich clothes and jewellery were considered a sure sign of royalist sympathies, but there were exceptions to this high-mindedness even among Oliver Cromwell's closest associates. General Harrison, a true Puritan, stated that 'gold and silver and worldly bravery did not become saints', but Colonel Hutchinson wore 'sad coloured cloth, trimmed with gold and silver points and buttons . . . pretty rich, but grave'.

The pendulum of fashion swings between extremes, marking time at the median point. The extreme of cumbersome garments and elaborate decoration under James I was replaced by the middle ground of the simple, elegant but rich dress of Charles I's court (*colour plate 2, facing page 25*) and superseded in turn by the extreme of Puritan sobriety. By the late 1650s the pendulum was swinging back towards more decoration and display as ribbons, lace and jewellery reappeared.

Some Puritans had left England to form new colonies in America where they hoped to create their own ideal society. Trading links were quickly established by astute English merchants, who saw these new colonies as a small but important market for their goods. Trade with other non-European countries was also growing, particularly with India, from where exotic Indian cottons were imported.

Menswear

DOUBLET

The 'peascod belly' padding was gradually replaced by two 'belly pieces' which were less distended pieces of stiffening on either inside front of the doublet. The sleeves were narrower with shoulder wings, and in the years after *c.*1618 the waistline rose, and the tabs were consequently longer, rather like a basque, but fewer in number. There were often decorative slashes across the chest, shoulders and upper arms in the late 1620s (*6*), or panes, which were strips of material like wide ribbons, caught at either end. By the late 1630s the waistline was very high with only four deep tabs, or with each back and each front cut in one piece with side gussets. In the 1640s and 1650s the doublet began to look more like a short jacket, as the two fronts and backs came only to waist level, with short tabs to cover the gap between doublet and breeches. The sleeves were shorter, often only elbow length. The usual method of fastening was by small buttons (*7*).

6   Charles I by G Honthorst 1628. The slashes on the upper body of the doublet and the panel sleeves reveal a good deal of the shirt; the falling ruff looks back to earlier seventeenth-century fashions in neck wear

7 Doublet *c*.1625-30. Linen, embroidered with linen thread in knot stitch and couching; the rising waistline is balanced by deep tabs; the row of small buttons is a feature of doublets at this date

JERKINS

Sleeveless jerkins were sometimes worn over the doublet in the early years of the century. Waistcoats, often padded, were worn under doublets for extra warmth.

BREECHES

The trunk-hose and canions, leg coverings extending from the base of the trunk hose to the knees, retained their place in men's fashions until the doublet began to lose its rigidity as the waistline rose. To balance this new line the breeches lengthened, and although still fairly full they were less stiff, but even this soft fullness diminished as the waistline rose even higher. By the early 1630s, long straight breeches, full at the waist, but narrow at the knee, were the usual fashion (*colour plate 2, facing page 25*). When the doublet began to change into something akin to a jacket in the early 1640s the breeches became shorter and began to widen into the 'petticoat' breeches of the 1650s. These were either separate legs over full, lavishly trimmed drawers (canons) or a short skirt over full bloomer breeches.

For the first 20 years or so of the seventeenth century breeches were still held to the doublet by points, but were gradually replaced by metal hooks inside the doublet waist to which the breeches were tied. The looser jacket style doublets of the 1650s were not attached to the breeches.

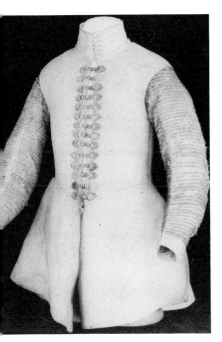

8   Buff coat *c*.1625-30. Although buff coats were used mostly for military pursuits, they always kept in step with changing fashions; metal clasps are used to fasten this example

OUTERWEAR

Circular capes, mainly shoulder-length or waist-length in the early years of the century, and lengthening as the doublet and breeches developed narrower lines, were very popular. Casaques or mandilions were worn for travelling; the latter was a cape with two fronts, two backs and two shoulder pieces which could be buttoned together to form a coat. The looser fitting jacket style doublet of the 1640s was developed from this easy and comfortable garment.

An important category of outer garments were the coats, doublets and jerkins which were made of buff (*8*). These were worn a good deal during the Civil War because of their protective thickness. Although they were heavy and rather rigid, they had features which kept in line with prevailing fashions.

UNDERWEAR AND INFORMAL DRESS

Linen shirts were a prominent feature during the fashion for slashed and paned doublets, although much less decorated than their sixteenth-century predecessors (*6*). The lace trimmed linen collars and cuffs which rose and fell, widened and diminished according to the fashion of the moment, were detachable.

Gowns were worn increasingly as an informal, undress fashion, although in the early years of the century older men still wore them in public for additional warmth over their doublets and breeches.

ACCESSORIES

Hats were an important male accessory, gradually increasing in width, and becoming less stiff. They were worn indoors and at meals on formal occasions until the 1680s, and were only removed in the presence of the king. Knitted stockings of silk or wool were worn for elegance or warmth respectively, but many men still wore cloth stockings, cut on the cross of the material, as they had done in the previous century. Footwear ranged from soft leather pumps to sturdy boots depending on the occasion, and gloves of equally soft leather could be plain or decorated according to the wearer's circumstances.

Women's clothes

GOWNS

Separate bodices and skirts, cut to suit the prevailing fashion, were worn throughout this period. In the early years of the century they were worn over the long bodied corsets and cartwheel farthingales. This fashion, much admired by James I's queen, retained its hold as a formal fashion until her death in 1619, but as early as *c*.1608 young women, tired of this cumbersome and restricting style of dress, had started to wear a natural waisted bodice and a gathered skirt, and this alternative, initially rather informal fashion, eventually developed a formal elegance of its own in the 1620s-1640s (*9*), (*10*) when its simplicity of line was complemented by the rich, glowing plain satins which Queen Henrietta Maria favoured.

OUTERWEAR

A variety of cloaks and mantles, often thickly lined, were worn in bad weather or for travelling.

UNDERWEAR AND INFORMAL DRESS

Over the smock was worn a farthingale and corsets or 'whalebone bodies' as they were called at the time. At the beginning of the century the farthingales were very full circles, but they diminished a little in size before finally disappearing in the early 1620s. The whalebone bodies were long and stiffly boned with a busk or central bone which pressed down onto the farthingale to produce the fashionable tilt. As waistlines rose to keep pace with menswear, the corsets became shorter-bodied, and under the softer skirts hip pads were worn in place of farthingales. Over these were worn petticoats of linen, silk or lightweight wool cloth.

Amongst the various informal fashions of the early part of this period, embroidered linen jackets remained popular (*11*). Long shawls were sometimes worn, or loose, full-length gowns. One popular garment with a confusing name was the nightgown. This was a type of loose one-piece house-dress or negligée which was much less stiffly boned than the fashionable bodices.

9 *above:* A Court lady, engraving by W Hollar *c.*1640. The graceful women's fashions of the 1620s and 30s still had a formal, stiffened bodice; the skirt was supported by hip pads; variations of this style of dress continued well into the 1680s (see *16*)

10 *above:* A merchant's daughter, engraving by W Hollar *c.*1640. Although dressed more modestly, with a shorter, less rigid bodice, a plain, closed skirt and a neat linen collar, the fashionable hairstyle and accessories would have met with the disapproval of the Puritans.

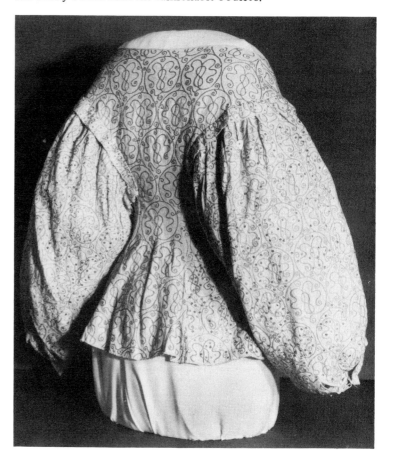

ACCESSORIES

There were many similarities between the accessories worn by men and women in the first half of the seventeenth century. Naturally there were differences of scale, but lace trimmed collars and ruffs, embroidered gloves, wide brimmed hats, and decorated stockings all bore many similarities to those worn by men (*colour plate 2 facing page 25*). Only their shoes had higher heels, and were often made of silk, as well as leather.

English materials

WOOL

The 'New Draperies' spread to the West Country early in the seventeenth century, and were produced there in addition to the more traditional broadcloths. There was a constant demand for fine worsteds and good quality broadcloths in Europe, and in later years, in the new settlements in America.

LINEN

Small quantities of linen continued to be produced in the north of England, but using imported yarn.

COTTON

Raw cotton was imported from the Middle East, and like all new and strange materials it was seen as a threat by the woollen weavers. The growth of this new industry, the main product of which was fustian, was mentioned in a petition of 1620: 'about twenty years ago past diverse people in this Kingdome, but chiefly in the countie of Lancashire, have found out the trade of making of other Fustians, made of a kind of Bombast or Downe . . . commonly called cotton wool . . . and also the Lynnen Yarne . . . There is at the least 40 thousand pieces of Fustian of this kind yearly made in England . . . and thousands of poor people set on working of these fustians'.

By 1640 the cotton industry was well established in the Manchester area, importing cotton through London from Smyrna and Cyprus, to spin, weave and dye into such materials as fustians, vermilions and dymities which were sold in London.

LACE

A small quantity of English lace was being made in Buckinghamshire by the 1630s.

11 *left:* **Bodice** *c.***1635-50. Linen embroidered in chain stitch with silver thread and spangles; this type of bodice could have been worked by many seventeenth-century needlewomen.**

Foreign materials

SILK

All silk materials were still imported from Italy and Spain, although a small quantity of plain silk came from France. Some English customers found the choice of imported silks available in London rather disappointing. In 1621 the diplomat Dudley Carleton noted that the choice of dress silks which could be bought in the Hague was wider than those in London, and that he knew of many Englishwomen who ordered their best dress materials from there.

LINEN

Various grades of linen, from the finest quality for shirts, smocks and collars, to the coarsest, for linings, were imported from the Low Countries and Germany.

COTTON

In 1600 a charter was granted to the East India Company to trade in, amongst other items, Indian painted cottons. These were imported, but initially they were used for furnishings rather than for clothing.

LACE

The most sophisticated and expensive lace still came from Italy, but a small quantity of cheaper lace came from the Low Countries, and towards the end of this period lace was being imported from France.

RIBBONS, BRAIDS, FRINGES

These came from Italy, Spain and France, and can often be identified by a place-name attached to the article.

Makers and construction

Men's and women's clothes continued to be made by tailors, as in the sixteenth century. The earliest surviving men's tailoring manuals, French and Spanish in origin, date from this period, but they do not herald any major advances in tailoring techniques. It was still all important to make the best use of expensive materials, and tailoring was concerned with the alteration of existing patterns to suit individual customers, and the shaping, gathering and pleating of material. Tailors also made corsets and farthingales for their female customers.

Articles such as hats, gloves, shoes and other accessories were made to order by the various specialist craftsmen. Linen items were made by the female members of a family (*11*), and in poorer or isolated households they probably also made other items of clothing, although journeymen tailors did not charge greatly for their services.

Shops

London continued to be the main centre for fashionable shopping, and many people would order their clothes from there, through a relative or friend, or make an occasional shopping trip themselves. The two main shopping areas in the capital were London Bridge and Cheapside. In 1633 the shops on the north side of London Bridge included eight haberdashers of small wares, six hosiers, five haberdashers of hats, three silkmen, two glovers, two mercers, two woollen drapers, one milliner, one shoemaker and one linen draper. Apart from these traders in new goods, the secondhand clothes trade continued to flourish.

English merchants quickly saw potential markets in the new settlements in America, and in 1625 two ships left Bristol with cargoes of 'hats of divers colours, apparel of coarse kersey and canvas ready-made, stockings, shoes' etc. As the quotation implies, it was possible to buy sturdy, basic garments ready-made, although alterations were likely to be made by the customers themselves.

Prices

1600	For a pair of silk stockings, 25s
1605	For the cloth to make a pair of stockings, 5s
1608	For Holland (linen) to make shirts, per ell, 13s 4d
1608	For a pair of shoes, 3s 6d
1613	For a cutwork band and cuffs, £6-£7
1621	For 10 yards of birdseye tiffany, 12s 6d
1623	For 3¼ yards of sad green cloth for a cloak, 52s 0d and for the baize to line it, 16s 0d

1628	For a coloured felt hat, lined with silk and with a band of gold and silver, 15s
1642	For black silk mohair, per yard, 5s 6d
1649	For 3 yards of watchet (blue) satin for a waistcoat, £1 13s 0d

Technical developments

After William Lee's death in France c.1610, his brother James Lee returned to England with all but one of his knitting frames. He installed these in Old Street Square in London, but later moved to Nottingham where he built more knitting frames. The industry continued, on a small scale, in London, where the framework knitters joined together to form a trade association. Higher speeds were gradually achieved, and additional articles, such as gloves and mittens, were produced.

Surviving costume

Although there are more surviving items of costume from this period, many of them still belong to the categories of incomplete garments or accessories. The widest range of items, including complete suits, are in the collection of the **Victoria and Albert Museum** in London; other museums with important, but incomplete, examples are:

Museum of London

Museum of Costume, Bath

Museum of Costume, Nottingham

Gallery of English Costume, Manchester

Museum and Art Gallery, Northampton (footwear only)

Other museums may have a few small items from this period, but the range is so limited that very little information can be gleaned from them.

1660-1719 Restoration and Change

The restoration of the monarchy in 1660 was the signal for a period of renewed social exuberance, and for changes in men's and women's fashions. It was once again possible to wear new styles, rich materials and frivolous accessories without exciting unfavourable comments.

Many exiled courtiers returned to England wearing the fashions of France or Holland. In the mid 1660s the English Court followed the French attempts to find a new style of menswear, and from this time onwards French fashions in dress and materials were influential throughout Europe. When the mantua was introduced into female dress in the 1670s it was a French fashion that was copied in England and elsewhere in Europe. Even the accession of William III and Mary II to the throne in 1689 and their political opposition to France did not prevent the English from copying and wearing French styles.

When England acquired its own silk industry in the 1680s it was due to an influx of refugee French Huguenot weavers and designers. They were quickly assimilated into the thriving English textile industry, which despite its constant anxiety about foreign imports, was able to see the importance of being able to offer an ever increasing range of home produced textiles. This fear of foreign goods led to the prohibition of the popular Indian printed cottons in the early years of the eighteenth century, but also prompted experiments with methods of cotton printing within the British Isles. English textile workers did not mind using imported yarn, just as long as the end product was their own.

One frustrating feature of this period is the shortage of illustrations of English fashionable dress. This is largely due to the artistic convention which portrayed sitters in undress. These informal garments reflect a contemporary desire for a more relaxed and timeless form of portraiture. Consequently, it is necessary to look at book illustrations, engravings and French fashion plates to find out what was actually worn, and the evidence does seem to imply a considerable dependence on French fashions.

Menswear

The last chapter foreshadowed the changing shape and character of the basic items of menswear which took place in the 1650s. The major change occurred in the mid to late 1660s when the short doublet lost all its original form and importance, and was finally replaced by the longer, loose-fitting coat.

A number of experiments took place to find an elegant and comfortable alternative to the extravagantly full petticoat breeches and short doublet which were fashionable when Charles II was restored to the monarchy in 1660 (12). The king took an active interest in these new fashions, and was one of the first to wear the new garments, which were described by the diarist Samuel Pepys in

THE KING
    &Equeries   Gentlemen Penſioners   Yeomen of th.
                             & Equeries

12   Procession of Charles II, print *c*.1661. The three young men to the left are dressed in the loose doublet-coat and full petticoat breeches which preceded the new style of suit; the lavish use of braid and ribbons was quite usual

October 1666 as ' . . . a long cassocke close to the body . . . and a coat over it.' In effect these two garments were a longer version of the loose doublet worn under a coat which had its origins in the earlier casaques and mandilions. These new styles quickly became fashionable, and Pepys, in spite of his limited means as a minor government official, quickly ordered himself a set. In his diary entry for 4 November 1666 he noted, 'My taylor's man brings my vest home, and coat to wear with it . . . so I rose and dressed myself, and I like myself mightily in it, and so do my wife.' Vest was yet another name for the 'cassocke'; both terms were eventually displaced by the word waistcoat.

COATS

When the coat first appeared it was a loose-fitting, rather shapeless garment, with two fronts, two backs and open seams from the hem to just below the waist. It had elbow-length sleeves, no collar, and it was fastened by buttons from the neck to the hem, although it was worn with few if any of the buttons done up. During the 1670s and 1680s it became closer fitting (*13*), then in the 1690s extra width was introduced into the coat skirts and into the sleeves (*14*). By the beginning of the eighteenth century the fullness in the skirts was arranged into side pleats (*15*), and by *c*.1715-1720 two pleats had appeared on either side of the centre back vent.

WAISTCOATS

These were similar in appearance to the coat, but narrower in line. Between *c*.1680 and 1700 the waistcoat sleeves were longer than coat sleeves, then they were turned back as cuffs before finally disap-

13 *above:* Coat *c.*1680. Doeskin embroidered with silver thread; the coat was fairly narrow by this date, but still rather shapeless; vertical pockets and rows of small buttons are always found on early coats.

pearing, except for informal wear when a sleeved waistcoat might be worn without a coat. More waistcoat buttons were done up.

BREECHES

These remained very full and highly decorated at first, but by the early 1690s all trimmings had disappeared, and they were narrower.

OUTERWEAR

Capes were worn for travelling, but gradually they were replaced by loose-fitting 'great' coats, which had started as a fashion for riding.

UNDERWEAR AND INFORMAL DRESS

Shirts were very full at the beginning of the 1660s, pouching over the breeches beneath the short doublet jacket. The sleeves were full and unnaturally long as they were intended to be worn with a puffed flounce above the wristband (*12*). Lace bands, and then cravats,

14 *bottom left:* Coat *c*.1690. Brown twilled wool with silk thread buttons; the wider coat skirts are balanced by wider and deeper cuffs.

15 *left:* Joseph Collet, wood sculpture by A Chinqua, 1716. The coat skirts have developed side pleats and the pockets are horizontal flaps; the waistcoat and breeches are a matching brocaded silk; the more formal line of the suit is matched by an elegant linen cravat, buckled shoes, a walking stick and a full bottomed wig

with matching or plain cuffs, were always detachable (*15*). Men started to wear drawers, although at first they were called 'breeches linings'. Nightshirts were always worn in bed, and covered by loose robes for informal wear.

ACCESSORIES

Decoration was added to clothes in the form of sashes, gloves, walking sticks and coloured stockings (*15*). Shoes were usually of leather, high-fronted and fastened with buckles. Hats were wide brimmed at the beginning of the period, and then three cornered; after 1680 they were only worn out of doors.

The most important male accessory was the wig. Wigs were worn from the 1660s onwards. At first they were full and long (*15*), but gradually variations in style and shape were introduced, so that by 1720 there were wigs to suit all tastes and occasions. Working men did not wear wigs as they were both expensive and cumbersome, but they grew their hair longer.

Women's clothes

The introduction of a new form of menswear was eventually matched by a similar development in women's dress, but at first the long stiff bodices and separate skirts of the 1650s continued to be fashionable, until the increasing discomfort caused by these rigid bodices led to the search for a less formal style.

GOWNS

16 Engraving from Sandford's *History of the Coronation of James II*, 1687. The men's coats are more elaborate versions of those in *14*; the women are dressed in ceremonial versions of the long bodied, oval necked gown with a trained skirt which was formal wear even after the introduction of the mantua

The formal, stiff-bodied gowns were always made in two pieces. The bodice was mounted on a heavily boned lining, and as the front became longer only this section was worn outside the skirt; the bodice tabs were worn inside the skirt waistband. These bodices usually had a low, oval neckline, and short, fairly full sleeves. Skirts were rather narrower than those of the 1650s, but constructed in the same way. In the 1660s an additional overskirt, open at the front, and with a long train, was worn (*16*). This overskirt was pulled up into side drapes in the 1670s and eventually formalised into folds around the hips which were held in place at the centre back.

A loose gown, called a *robe de chambre*, was increasingly worn in the 1670s as a respite from the formal gowns. It was worn over a less rigid bodice, and from the combination of these two garments a new style of dress developed. It was called a mantua, and was an important item of female dress for over 100 years.

MANTUAS

The *robe de chambre* was a T-shaped garment, with one back piece, and one front, and held at the waist by a sash. Gradually this simple garment evolved into a more stylish dress. The material was pleated into several folds to create a fitted bodice, and the pleats were held at the waist by a belt. By the end of the century there were only two pleats on either side of an open-fronted bodice, and two pleats on either side of the centre back; the pleats were stitched to the waist, and the skirt was taken back in folds as the earlier overskirt had been. The sleeves were cut separately, and were elbow-length with a turn-back cuff. The bodice was unboned, but it was worn over stays which either had a decorated front panel, or were covered by a stomacher which was a wedge-shaped panel pinned into position, or crossed over with bands of ribbons or bows. By the late 1680s the skirt had widened and was supported by a padded roll or small frame.

Once the basic structure of the mantua had evolved, it quickly became the most popular item of female dress, with its combination of elegance and comfort. Variations were introduced in the width of the sleeves; and the decoration of the bodice and skirt. The skirt grew wider and by *c*.1711 the skirt was emphasised even more as it was worn over a wide hoop.

OUTERWEAR

Loose short jackets were worn over mantuas; but the main item of outdoor clothing was a long cloak, often with a hood. For riding women wore a man's coat, a cravat and a cocked hat, and sometimes this costume was worn for travelling.

UNDERWEAR AND INFORMAL DRESS

The smock retained the wide, low cut neckline of the 1640s and 1650s, and until the mantua became an established fashion, parts of the smock's neckline and full sleeves could be seen (*17*). Stays were heavily boned, but became shorter under mantuas. Petticoats came in a wide variety of materials, and were full length or mid-calf length. In the 1690s Mary Evelyn described ' . . . short under Petticoats pure fine, some of Japan Stuff, some of Chine . . .' and ' . . . another quilted wide and red, with a broad Flanders lace below.' For informal wear the *robe de chambre* was retained.

ACCESSORIES

Women wore or carried many small decorative items, high heeled shoes, coloured stockings, elbow-length suede or kid gloves and mittens, fans, small bags, muffs and fur tippets (*18*). On their heads they wore small lace caps which became tall, tiered lace confections in the late 1680s and 1690s. These diminished into small round caps in the early years of the eighteenth century.

17 Woman's smock *c*.1700-10. White linen; the simple shape of this basic undergarment changed only in details, like the width and form of the sleeves and neckline

English materials

WOOL

The majority of the population continued to wear clothes made from woollen cloth, and men of fashion quickly realised that the new coat and vest would look as elegant in fine wool cloth as it did in silks and velvets. Fashionable women rarely wore wool except when it was made up into a riding habit, and these were often made from a wool and silk mixture. These mixtures of wool with silk or linen were very popular.

To meet the growing demand for wool cloth at home and abroad, it was necessary to import Spanish and Irish wool for use as weft yarn.

LINEN

The best organised area of linen production was in the north of England, around Manchester, where Scottish, Irish or continental yarn was carded and spun by cottage workers, and then professionally woven, finished and dyed in local workshops.

COTTON

The production of fustian continued in the areas of Lancashire where linen was woven.

LACE

This was produced in parts of South Devon, and in the East Midlands counties of Buckinghamshire, Northamptonshire and Bedfordshire. It could not match the quality of imported French or Flemish lace; it was a commodity for people who could not afford expensive foreign lace. In 1697 the importing of foreign lace was prohibited by Act of Parliament, but this aroused opposition in the Low Countries to English wool exports, and the Act was amended to ban only French lace.

SILK

The English silk industry was very small at the beginning of this period and only produced small goods, chiefly ribbons. However, Louis XIV's persecution of the French Protestants, many of whom were weavers, led to a dispersal of these craftsmen to England and Holland. A number of French silk weavers settled in the Spitalfields area of London, and were soon producing quantities of fine silks.

Foreign materials

SILK

The Italian and Spanish silk industries were gradually eclipsed by the French silk industry in the second half of the seventeenth century. Louis XIV took an active interest in native French industries which could provide fine quality luxury goods. During his reign the French Court became famous throughout Europe for its elegance, and many other countries began to import its imaginatively designed and finely made goods. French silks quickly found favour with the English. The Italian and Spanish silk industries were more conservative, and their silks, although still worn, did not keep pace with the new ideas that flowed constantly from the young, lively French designers and weavers.

Lightweight silks were imported from India and China by the East India Company, and were popular enough to be included in the 1701 ban (see section on cotton below).

LINEN

The finest quality linen continued to be imported from the Netherlands.

COTTON

The English trading links with India gradually led to a certain Europeanisation of the designs of printed cotton materials, which when they had first arrived in England had appeared very exotic. This Europeanisation was fairly subtle, so that the designs still met the taste for unusual goods and novelties which was a feature of post-Restoration England.

The finest Indian cottons, or chintzes as they were called, were painted, but there were cheaper printed versions. The bright, fast colours and their low price ensured their success, but this success led to opposition from English wool and silk weavers who saw these goods as a threat, and in 1701 they achieved a legal ban on the household use and wear of ' . . . all wrought silks, Bengals and stuffs mixed with silk or herba, of the manufacture of China, Persia or the East Indies, and all calicoes, painted, dyed, printed or stained there.'

Naturally, ingenious merchants tried to find methods of circumventing this ban, and the success of these attempts can be judged by the wording of a second ban in 1721 which extended the prohibition to ' . . . any callicoes stitched or flowered in foreign parts with any colour or colours or with coloured flowers.'

LACE

This was imported from both France and the Low Countries, and was very costly. It was much used as a trimming, and was also made up into cravats, scarves, shoulder capes and aprons (18). Although these types were less heavy than Italian laces they were still densely patterned.

In 1675 Charles II ordered his subjects not to wear foreign lace, and in 1697 a ban on French and Flemish lace was enacted.

Makers and construction

Tailors maintained their position as the makers of both male and female formal clothes until the late seventeenth century. The introduction of the mantua allowed female mantua makers to establish themselves as the main makers of women's clothes. The simple shape of these garments did not require the skill and experience of a tailor. All that the mantua maker had to do was to drape, pleat and pin the lengths of material to suit the individual customer.

The mantua maker was originally a seamstress, providing a professional service for making men's shirts, ruffs and cravats, and the *robes de chambre* from which the mantua evolved. The blurred line between the work of the tailor and that of the seamstress is indicated in Randle Holmes' *Academy of Armory*, published in 1688, where he states 'The Seamster or Seamstry work follows next in order to adorn the Head, Hands and Feet, as the other [taylor] is for the covering of the Body; nay very often the Seamster occupieth the room and place of a Taylor in furnishing the Nobility and Gentry with such conveniences as serve the whole body, especially in the Summer Season.'

Tailors did not lose complete control over women's fashions. They continued to provide the more complicated and structural items, namely stays and riding habits. However, they were fully occupied devising new and more elegant forms for men's suits, and do not seem to have resented the rise of the mantua maker.

Ready made clothing for both sexes was becoming more available, although it was usually limited to ranges of informal or loose-fitting items and accessories, but Bourne and Harper's warehouse in Catherine Street, Covent Garden, also sold riding habits and cloaks.

Many women continued the tradition of making linen underwear, informal garments and accessories, and of spinning their own yarn or wool. The sophisticated London methods were far from usual elsewhere in England.

Shops

This period saw considerable expansion in the size of towns, the variety of goods on sale, and the movement of goods throughout the country. Many merchants began to only trade in goods instead of being involved in their production, but the expanding market was able to absorb increasing numbers of both makers and sellers.

In London the main shopping areas moved west from the City and were established in the Strand and in Covent Garden. Although the widest range of fashion goods was found in London, shops in other parts of the country were attracting favourable notice from sophisticated travellers. In 1699 when Celia Fiennes visited Newcastle she recorded her impression that 'Their shops are good and of distinct trades, not selling many things in one shop as is the custom in most country towns and cities.'

Country areas were fairly well served by fairs and markets where both wholesale and retail goods could be bought by local merchants and private customers respectively. The travelling salesmen who provided many of the small accessories and trimmings for customers in isolated areas, were licensed in 1697 as a public safeguard against disreputable pedlars.

Prices

1662	For a woman's silk gown and satin petticoat, including all materials and the tailor's time, £1 9s
1662	For a man's secondhand velvet cloak, £8 10s
1664	For a cloth suit and coat, £17
1693	For a pair of man's linen drawers, 4s
1693	For a linen waistcoat, 10s
1694	For an imported lace apron, £17
1703	For blue wool cloth, per yard, 18s
1711	For a ready made gown of rich brocade, 6gns
1713	For mixed worsted and silk cloth, per yard, 1s 3d
1719	For a coloured cloth suit, £2 8s 3d

Technical developments

The fashion for Indian printed cottons lead to experiments in England with methods of cotton printing.

1676 William Sherwin, an engraver of West Ham, took out a patent for 14 years on ' . . . the invention of a new and speedy way for producing broad calico, which being the only true way of the East India printing and stayning such kind of goods.'

1690 A French Protestant refugee established the first English calico printing factory at West Sheen, near London, and by 1700 calico printing was flourishing in many parts of south east England where there were good supplies of water.

The newly established silk weaving industry in Spitalfields had to import expensive thrown silk, until John Lombe discovered the secret of this closely guarded method during a visit to Italy.

1718 John Lombe's brother Thomas was granted a patent for ' . . . a new invention of three sorts of engines never before made or used in Great Britain, one to wind the finest raw silk, another to spin and the other to twist the finest Italian raw silk into organzine in great perfection, which was never before done in this country.'

1719 The Lombe brothers built a factory on the banks of the River Derwent in Derby, and they began to install machinery which was driven by a water wheel. The early machinery was very bulky and required a large building to house it.

Surviving costume

A small number of complete items of both sexes survive from this period, and can be seen, from time to time, in various English museums and private collections. There are also a number of incomplete items and accessories, bodices, waistcoats, shirts, embroidered caps, shoes, boots, fans, all of which add to the total picture of the taste of the men and women of the late seventeenth and early eighteenth centuries.

Unfortunately all that is afforded to us is an incomplete picture, as the items which do survive are not spread evenly over the 60 years.

Collections which include important items, although not in any quantity, are:

Museum of Costume, Bath

Verney Collection, Claydon House, Buckinghamshire

Museum of London

Victoria and Albert Museum, London

Gallery of English Costume, Manchester

Central Museum and Art Gallery, Northampton (footwear only)

Clive House Museum, Shrewsbury (one very fine mantua of *c*.1706-8)

1720-1789 A Wider World

Fashions began to change more quickly in the eighteenth century. Increased travel at home and abroad, for both business and pleasure, produced a more sophisticated population whose demand for more exotic and varied goods could be matched by the goods provided as a result of the growth in overseas trade, and by the variety of materials which flowed from the looms of the expanding textile industry. Although the main items worn by men and women throughout this period were based on late seventeenth century developments, the suit and the mantua, they were constantly evolving into more elegant and refined versions of these garments. New materials, trimmings and accessories appeared with an almost seasonal regularity.

This interest in novelties and change poses one of the major problems for the student of costume history, that of the abundance of different names which were given to styles of dress, materials and trimmings. This practice accelerated in the nineteenth century, and new names for familiar garments or trimmings appeared nearly every year. Today we hardly ever bother to master the changing names of fashions or materials. We know that something is made from a natural or a synthetic fibre or a combination of both, and we buy dresses, suits and coats using these basic terms rather than resorting to the fashion writer's jargon. This commonsense approach can, quite reasonably, be applied to eighteenth- and nineteenth-century clothes and materials. All materials were either wool or linen or cotton or silk, or a combination of two of these yarns; and most items of dress can be identified in a similarly rational way. Throughout this book only the most important contemporary names are used.

The English were equally rational about their clothes during the eighteenth century. Although the pendulum of fashion swung towards the extremes of exaggeration and fussiness at both ends of the period, for nearly 40 years, between the late 1730s and the late 1770s, fashions were elegant and reasonably comfortable. An element of informality was introduced by the adoption of country styles and the use of lighter materials, an English development which was observed critically, and then copied by the exquisites of the French court.

English children were the first to wear clothes which allowed them freedom of movement and an identity of their own, instead of turning them into miniature adults (*colour plate 5, facing page 49*). Girls wore plain, high-waisted cotton or muslin dresses; boys wore pantaloons, or pantaloons and an attached jacket, called a skeleton suit. These children of the post 1760 era recalled this comfort and freedom when they became adults, and tried to find a similar freedom in the easier, less constricting fashions of the 1770s and 1780s.

Towards the end of the eighteenth century men's clothes became plainer and were made from more practical wool cloths rather than rich silks. This change is one reflection of a more serious approach to their work as landowners, politicians, merchants and manufacturers which characterised many men at this time. Fine clothes were kept for special occasions, but even these were less rich than formerly. At this point in history the clothes worn by men and women ceased to develop along parallel lines; they diverged to emphasise their differing roles; with women cast in the role, unconsciously at first, of finely, but impractically dressed social ornaments.

Menswear

Throughout this period the most important items in a man's wardrobe were the coat, waistcoat and breeches which formed his suit. Sometimes all three pieces matched, but later in the century three different materials were used, carefully selected to complement each other (*colour plate 5, facing page 49*).

COATS

Coat skirts continued to widen in the 1720s and 1730s, as extra back and side pleats were introduced (*19*), and usually contained an inner stiffening, such as buckram, to hold the shape. By the mid 1740s the width was decreasing; the coat fronts started to curve back and the sleeves lengthened and grew narrower (*colour plate 4*). In the 1760s a narrow standing collar was added. The extra back pleats disappeared, the side pleats were fewer in number; the front edges sloped away, and the collar increased in height to produce the narrow, elegant coat of the 1770s (*20*).

The country cousin of this formal coat was the frock. It was simpler and looser in construction; double or single breasted with a turn-down collar. It was a comfortable alternative to the bulky, expensive formal coats of the 1730s and 1740s, and quickly became a favourite informal garment. In the late 1770s a double breasted version of the frock underwent a number of important changes. The top buttons were left undone to allow the fronts to fall back into revers, and the front was cut horizontally at the waist to allow more

Colour plate

4   Sir Thomas Robinson by F van der Mijn 1750. As the coat skirts sloped away, more of the waistcoat was revealed; the **plain satins**, relieved by only a small amount of embroidery and lace, display the restrained elegance of mid eighteenth-century menswear; Sir Thomas wears the bobwig favoured by older men

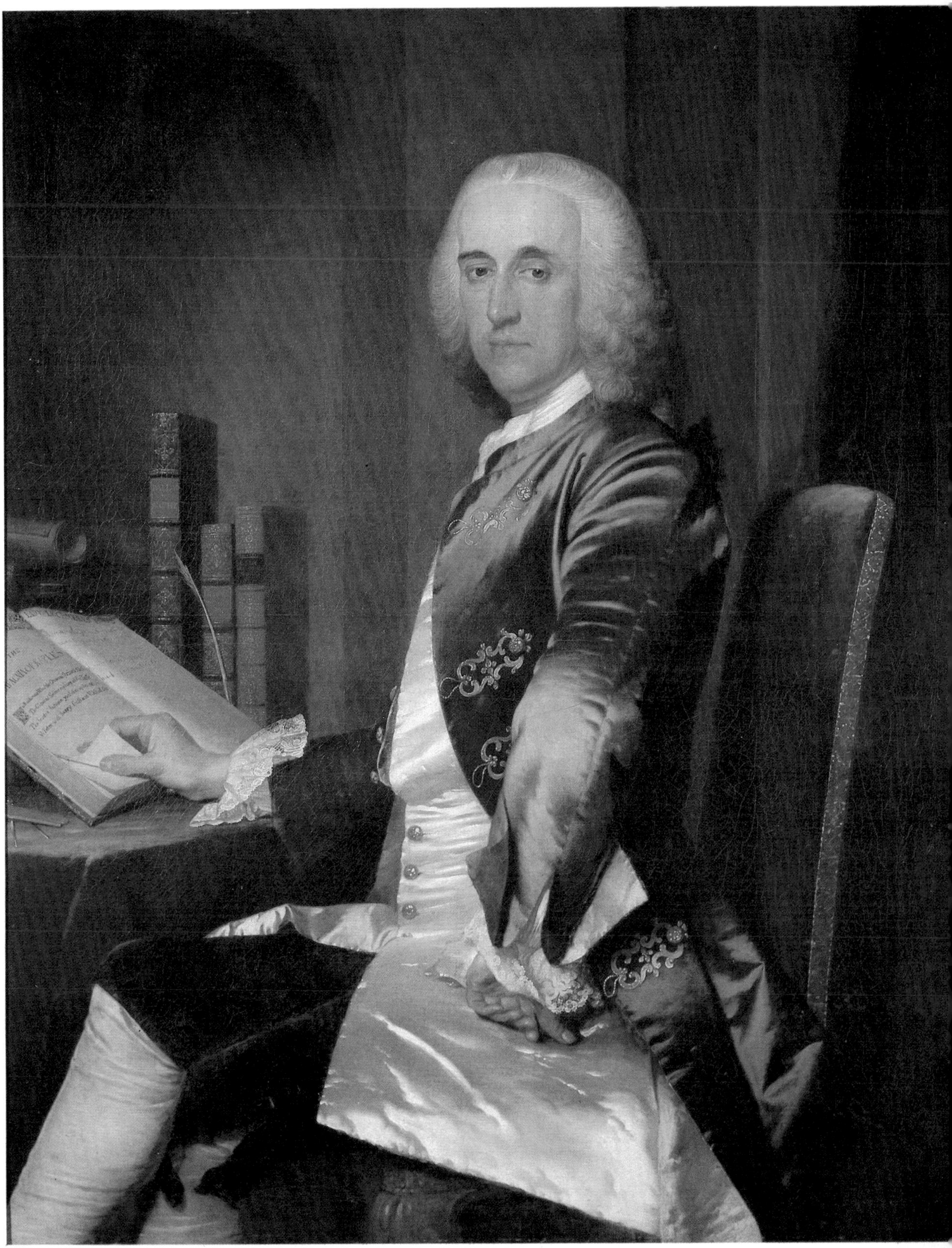

19 Frederick, Prince of Wales and his sisters by P Mercier 1733. The prince is wearing a full skirted coat and matching waistcoat and a fashionable tie-wig; his sisters are dressed in closed robes, a type of mantua, and modest linen kerchiefs and caps

Colour plate

5 The Sharp Family by J Zoffany, 1779-81. The simplicity of the men's clothes is in marked contrast to the richly decorated silk dresses of the women. The desire for a more restrained elegance is reflected in the tailored riding habits worn by two of the women, while the simple muslin dress worn by the elder girl foreshadows the softer, less ornate dresses worn by women in the next two decades

freedom of movement. A refined version of this style appeared in the 1780s, cut with wide revers and a high collar and given large buttons. The narrow skirts were caught back, all side pleats were eliminated and the tails were elongated to form the first tailcoats for fashionable town wear. This fashion was popular with young men, but older men continued to wear the conservative styles of their youth, and the earlier style of coat remained the only acceptable dress for Court functions.

WAISTCOATS

Broadly speaking, these changed about as frequently as the coats under which they were worn. Waistcoat fronts curved, and the whole garment became shorter in the 1720s, and continued to shorten until by the 1780s it was waist-length to match the frock coat (21). Collars were introduced in the 1760s and kept pace with the height of coat collars. In the 1780s double breasted waistcoats with revers were worn with frock coats.

BREECHES

The breeches of the 1720s to the 1750s were loose and comfortable with a simple fly fastening, but as waistcoats grew shorter and breeches became more visible they were cut to fit more closely over

49

the thighs and knees (20). The fly front was covered by a more modest 'fall', a flap which buttoned over the fly opening.

21 Waistcoat 1775-85. White satin embroidered in silks and net appliqué; delicate floral embroidery was a typical feature of waistcoats at this date. They were worked in waistcoat shaped panels; unmade examples can be seen in various museums

20 Coat and waistcoat 1770-75. Fawn wool cloth embroidered with silver thread and spangles; the narrow cut away coat and the shorter waistcoat are matched by slimmer fitting breeches

OUTERWEAR

Greatcoats and thick capes were popular until the 1750s. Later in the century the popularity of four-in-hand driving led to the use of a sophisticated version of a coachman's greatcoat with its layered capes.

UNDERWEAR AND INFORMAL DRESS

Very little of the shirt was visible, and it was the neckwear — cravats and bands, with matching cuffs, often decorated with fine lace — which could be seen. Drawers became less full as the breeches fitted more tightly. Gowns were worn informally, but they were more fitted, with button fastenings instead of sashes. Sleeved waistcoats became less fashionable for informal wear and were only worn by older men.

ACCESSORIES

The most important male accessory throughout much of this period was the wig. Wigs came in a number of styles for informal and formal wear. The full, longer wigs of the early years of the century were replaced by tie wigs in the 1720s. These had a single tail or 'queue' which was held back from the face by a ribbon (*19*) or contained in a wig-bag. Older men, and various professions such as the Law and the Church retained the longer, curled bob-wig (*colour plate 4, facing page 48*). On formal occasions wigs were heavily powdered.

Other accessories were fairly plain, as a contrast to the decorated suits of the early part of the period, and as a reflection of the desire for a more contrived simplicity in the later period. The only flamboyant features were the buttons, buckles and other items of jewellery which contained fine gemstones or paste.

Women's clothes

The two items of women's dress which influenced the fashionable silhouette were the stays and the hoop. The way in which they moulded the upper part of the torso and exaggerated the lower half are the key to understanding changes in female fashions.

DRESSES

Two main styles of dress were worn throughout this period. The first was the mantua, called the *robe à l'Anglaise* by foreigners, and the second was the sack, a French fashion. Other styles of dress, with confusing names, appeared from time to time, but, in essence, all dresses were variants of these two main types.

The mantua skirt widened and flattened in the 1720s and 1730s as the hoop changed shape. At first the skirts were pleated back over the hoop and held by cords, while the long train was looped up. Later, the skirt was folded round the hoop sides in the late 1730s, until, in its final form the mantua was only a bodice with side basques and a long narrow back train over a full underskirt. This final version was retained for Court wear, but for ordinary wear it was replaced by a bodice joined to an open-fronted floor length skirt. This style appeared in the late 1730s (*22*) and with certain changes, retained its popularity for over 40 years (*23*). By the late 1740s the simplicity of this style was relieved by the application of decoration down the bodice and skirt fronts, and the sleeves were finished with hanging flounces instead of pleated cuffs.

The next major change took place in the 1770s when the bodice lost its pleats and closed at the front. The back pleats moved to the centre back and became so narrow that they were replaced by seams. The skirt was narrowly pleated and extended into a shallow train which could be looped up into loose puffs. The sleeves were tightly fitting and extended to the wrist in the 1780s.

22 Mantua *c.*1740, stomacher 1730-40, petticoat 1730-50. An open robe of cream brocaded silk is worn over a quilted cream satin petticoat and a linen stomacher embroidered with silks and metal thread. This style of dress with differing skirt widths, was popular for nearly 40 years

All these dresses had matching or contrasting underskirts, some of which were quilted for extra warmth and bulk (*22*). The dresses fastened over a stomacher, or with flat bows or kerchief points held in place with pins (*24*). The sack evolved from a loose, undress garment with pleats at the front and the back, which hung in an unfitted line from the shoulders. It was always worn over a hoop. By the time it became fashionable in England in the 1740s, the front bodice was constructed in a similar manner to a mantua bodice, but the back hung free below two box pleats. The sleeves fitted to the elbow and were trimmed with flounces. The sack was always open-fronted, but the stomacher and petticoat often matched the dress. Once this fashion had been adopted by Englishwomen it became as popular as the mantua, and its construction changed to keep pace with the taste for narrower fitted bodices and smaller hoops. By the

23 Mantua *c*.1769. An open robe of pink and green striped brocaded silk with a lawn kerchief and sleeve frills. The simple, elegant line of these dresses suited rich, patterned silks and delicate lawn or lace accessories

1770s front pieces, which buttoned together, had replaced stomachers, and the long train was looped up. In the 1780s the sack was worn only on the most formal of occasions.

The next major changes came from France. In the early 1780s Queen Marie Antoinette was wearing a dress called, in her honour, the *chemise de la reine*. It was a full, loose-bodied dress of fine, Indian muslin, cut like a smock (the French for smock is *chemise*) which was held into the waist by a wide sash, with ribbon ties holding the full sleeves into the arms. Its origins can be found in the light, loose-fitting dresses worn by Creole women in the West Indies. When it appeared in France and then in England it was recognised as the most informal style of dress ever worn by fashionable women.

OUTERWEAR

Short jackets, loose-fitting in the earlier part of the period, and narrower in the latter part, were popular with women of all classes. Capes and cloaks were worn for travelling. In the 1770s a driving or carriage coat, similar to a man's greatcoat, became fashionable.

52

24 Mantua 1760-65. Open robe and matching petticoat of cream brocaded silk, with am embroidered lawn apron, kerchief and sleeve frills; the flat, wide brimmed hat protected the face from sunshine

25 Stays 1740-60. Pale blue woollen damask, boned between each row of stitching, and lined with linen; such stays were worn under dresses like those in *22* and *24*

UNDERWEAR AND INFORMAL DRESS

Smocks with low necklines were still the principal undergarments. Stays were long-bodied and low-fronted in the 1720s (*25*), but gradually shortened in the 1770s and 1780s to produce stays which could be worn under the rising waistlines of the late 1780s. Hoops were worn for most of this period, but were at their widest in the 1730s and 1740s. They came in two varieties, a full hoop or two separate paniers, one for each side; both types tied around the waist. In the 1780s hoops were gradually replaced by small hip pads (*26*) as the dresses became softer and lighter in construction.

THE BUM SHOP.

26 Cartoon by T Rowlandson 1785.
The softer, high-waisted fashions of the
1780s emphasised a pouter-pigeon bust
and rounded hips; this cartoon pokes fun
at the methods used to achieve this
effect

ACCESSORIES

Women rarely wore wigs, although they powdered their hair for
formal occasions, and built it up over false pieces in the 1770s and
1780s (*colour plate 5, facing page 49*). They usually wore caps, or
arrangements of artificial flowers and ribbons on their heads. Hats
were important as they protected the complexion from sunshine;
consequently they were often wide brimmed (*24*), although their
shape and the depth of the crown altered according to the prevailing
fashion.

Lace was an important feature of dress, as a trimming or for
shoulder capes and shawls. Small aprons were popular, and varied in
type from densely embroidered silks (*27*) to the finest cottons.
Elbow-length gloves and mittens of the softest pastel coloured kid or
silk were popular, and fans were an indispensable formal accessory.

English materials

WOOL

Men of all classes wore wool suits, and the frock coat was invariably
made from a woollen cloth. Women rarely wore wool if they could
afford to follow fashion, but they sometimes chose calimancoes,
which were glazed satin weave worsteds printed with similar designs
to fashionable woven silks. The main centre for calimancoes was
Norwich, from where they were exported to European and American
markets.

Production of wool cloth was maintained at a high level as there
was a constant and growing demand for a wide variety of qualities
and weights of cloth for the home and foreign markets.

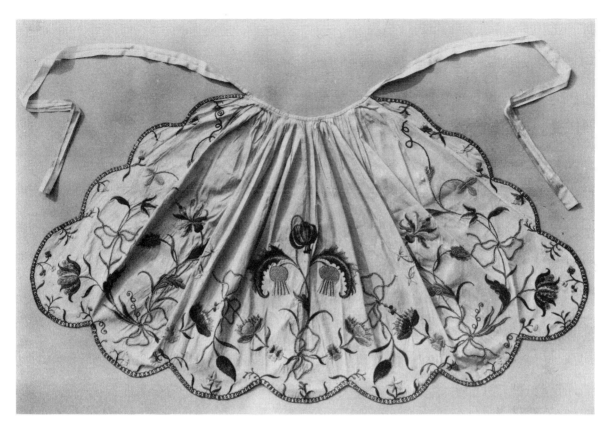

27 *above:* Apron 1730-50. Cream silk embroidered with coloured silks; aprons were a popular semi-formal fashion throughout the eighteenth century

28 *right:* Women's shoes 1700-30. Footwear followed the fashion for strongly patterned embroideries and brocaded silks early in the century; the clog in the foreground protected the shoe from the dirt and rubbish in the streets

LINEN

The prohibition of all printed cottons for home use, whether British or foreign in origin, which was enacted in 1721, gave a great boost to the linen industry. Printers turned their attention to linen, cotton and linen or silk and cotton mixtures. Printed linens became increasingly popular. They were cheap, attractive and easy to launder, and by the 1770s and 1780s well suited to the new, lighter dress styles. Linens were sent to London for printing until competent printers were trained in the areas close to the production of the cloth. Various printing techniques were used, and printed linens or mixtures were produced in Aberdeen and Edinburgh in the 1720s, in Glasgow from 1738, in Bolton from 1751, in Ireland in the mid 1750s, in Bamber Bridge and Carlisle in the early 1760s, and throughout Lancashire from the mid 1760s onwards.

COTTON

The cotton manufacturers were not deterred by the 1721 Act. They produced plain cottons, mixed materials and introduced new weaves and effects. A cotton velvet was developed in Lancashire, and ribbed cotton velvets, corduroys and fustians were produced in considerable quantities for country clothes and working people's dress.

Fine cotton muslins and lawns were produced in Paisley from the 1760s, and these almost transparent materials were much used for neckwear and dress accessories. At first linen thread was used, but fine cotton thread replaced it in the 1780s.

In 1774 the ban on printed cottons of English manufacture was lifted, and well designed prints quickly regained favour.

The use of cotton thread for knitting enabled knitted cotton stockings to be in production by the 1730s. At first they were made of imported Indian yarns, but knitted on silk stocking frames in Nottingham.

SILK

The Spitalfields silk industry was able to meet the demands of the home market by 1730. It produced fine brocaded silks, plain silks and silk/worsted mixtures. Designs followed the French taste until the early 1740s, and then, for over 20 years, they reflected contemporary English interest in botanical specimens with their accurate representations of flowers and plants (*24*). From the mid 1760s French designs were popular again.

Between 1720 and 1750 stiff, figured silks with small patterns were specially woven to suit the elegant, wide-skirted coats, waistcoats and breeches. When a fashion appeared which favoured heavily decorated coat fronts, with complementary decoration on the back skirts, pockets and cuffs, special coat lengths were woven with the decoration in place.

In the late eighteenth century silk weaving was established in Macclesfield, Glasgow and Manchester, but output was limited to small goods such as handkerchiefs, silk gauze and low grade silks.

Foreign materials

This was a period of prohibition. Protection for the thriving British textiles industries was considered of national importance. The import duty on goods which were not banned was very high. Naturally such bans and import duty did not destroy demand. Breaking the law was an added excitement for many people, and smuggling, on an organised level, and by individuals, was a feature of eighteenth-century life. English travellers often brought back contraband goods from abroad, but few could compete with Lady Hodernesse, whose haul of smuggled goods in 1764 contained, it was said, 114 French gowns and pieces of silk.

The most important prohibition, which were in force throughout this period, were:

1697 Ban on imported Flemish and French lace (the former was exempted after a battle with Flemish importers of English wool cloth)

1721 Ban on imported Indian printed and embroidered cottons and silks

1749 Ban on imported metal embroidery, gold and silver lace, fringe and allied goods

1766 Ban on imported French silks

Makers and construction

By 1720 the division between men's tailors and women's mantua makers was well established. Tailors still made women's riding habits and stays (*26*), but all their other garments were made by mantua makers or milliners.

Although the earliest English tailoring manual was not published until 1796, it is possible to judge what skills were demanded of an eighteenth-century tailor by reading the article 'L'Art du Tailleur', which appeared in the encyclopaedia *Description des Arts et Metiers* in 1769. In essence, the various stages in the making of a suit were: taking of measurements, 19 in all for the three garments, taking note of any physical defects which required extra padding and stiffening and cutting the material with the minimum of waste from existing patterns adjusted to the customer's own measurements. Then strengthening material, buckram, padding and the lining were inserted; the buttonholes were stitched and pockets placed, then the final stitching and pressing was done. The two particular skills emphasised by the author were cutting and pressing, ' . . . the latter process giving the garment the elegant and durable shape it should have.' By the 1770s breeches makers were working independently. This division had developed because they worked with leather for riding breeches or working clothes, and this involved a different craft process. However, when cloth, corduroy and hard wearing cotton materials replaced leather, breeches makers were allowed to turn their skills to these new materials, and by the 1790s it was considered that they made better breeches than most tailors.

The skills of the mantua maker were considered of far less note than those of the tailor. In 'L'Art du Tailleur', she is described as having no special tools: ' a thimble, some needles, some thread, some silk, a pair of scissors and a flat-iron are sufficient for her work.' This is not an altogether unfair description, because very little cutting was required. The mantua or sack was constructed on a linen bodice lining which was shaped to fit over the stays, but the rest of the dress was put together from the outside. This was inevitable because the patterns of expensive brocaded silks had large repeats which had to be carefully aligned (*24*). This simple construction, with widths of material joined at the selvage edges and held with running stitches, is always a surprise to modern dressmakers. In fact it met both of the major requirements of eighteenth-century customers, that the dress should look magnificent, but that it should also be easy to unpick and remodel. The neat stitching and scrupulous finish of linen undergarments was not copied by dressmakers until the lighter, cheaper materials of the 1770s and 1780s made this practical in both dressmaking and financial terms.

The work of the mantua makers was complemented by that of the milliners. The latter provided the exquisite trimmings which decorated dresses from the late 1740s onwards, as well as providing the latest styles in caps, ruffles and headdresses.

The complicated embroidery which distinguished formal dresses was also carried out separately.

Women who could afford the services of a mantua maker rarely made their own dresses, but they did do an immense amount of embroidery and fine sewing. Occasionally they embroidered widths of silk or muslin which the mantua maker would make into a dress, but their usual work was concerned with the embroidery and construction of small accessories: aprons, caps, ruffles, tuckers and handkerchiefs. Patterns for this type of work were published in the *Lady's Magazine* from 1770 onwards.

Shops

As towns grew in size, and roads and transport improved, the range of shops outside the large cities increased, but many men and women still preferred to order their finest clothes from London.

Tradesmen competed for custom by advertising in the newspapers, by issuing decorative trade cards and bills, and by placing distinctive signs outside their shops. Shop windows were also arranged in a way that might attract customers. When Sophie de la Roche visited London in 1786 she noticed that ' . . . there is a cunning device for showing women's materials. They hang down in folds behind the fine, high windows so the effect of this or that material, as it would be in a woman's dress, can be studied'.

When a customer stepped inside a shop to meet a shopkeeper or an assistant, who, according to *The London Tradesman*, 1747, should ' . . . speak fluently, though not elegantly, [be able] to entertain the ladies; and to be master of a handsome bow and cringe . . .' she did not expect to see prices marked on goods, or to pay in cash. An exception to this rule, which foreshadowed trading practices which were not generally observed for over 100 years, was Palmer's haberdashery shop on London Bridge. According to Robert Owen, who worked there as a young man, 'It was a house established, and I believe the first, to sell at small profit and for ready money only . . . . Not much time was allowed for bargaining, a price being fixed for everything and, compared with other houses, cheap. If any demur was made or much hesitation, the article asked for was withdrawn and another customer attended to.' Palmers traded in this manner from about 1750, but the more leisurely practice of discussion and bargaining continued elsewhere.

Fairs were still an important feature in country trading in the early part of this period, but decreased in importance as more shops were established in the provinces. Travelling tradesmen increased in numbers as factory production in Scotland, the north of England and the Midlands became more sophisticated. 'Manchester men' carried goods from the factories to shopkeepers throughout the country, and occasionally, sold directly to the public. Their retail counterparts were the Scottish drapers who travelled from house to house in poor areas, selling mainly on credit, with a stock in trade of cheap factory goods not easily found outside the newly industrialised areas.

Prices

1723   For a quilted petticoat, £3 19s 2d

1725   For a brown suit with silver trimmings, £17

1731   For pink silk damask, per yard, 7s

1739   For a man's red damask gown, £4 18s

1753   For silk brocaded with gold and silver thread, per yard, £4

1764   For a cloth suit, £4 8s

1766   For a ready made yellow and white linen dress, £1 4s

1772   For 6 ells of Irish linen to make 2 shirts, 16s 3d

1781   For 5½ yards of chintz to make a dress, £1 14s

1783   For pink lustring to make a petticoat, per yard, 5s 9d

Technical developments

Major advances were made in the field of textile machinery. New inventions enabled manufacturers to produce large quantities and new varieties of textiles. These goods ranged from the cheapest cottons to the most expensive wool cloths, and they were exported in considerable amounts. The main developments were in the area of cotton production.

PRODUCTION OF COTTON

1733   John Kay patented the fly-shuttle which increased the speed of weaving by eliminating the movements by hand of the weft shuttle thread; this invention was in general use by 1750.

1738   Lewis Paul took out a patent on a spinning machine.

1741-42   James Hargreaves devised the spinning jenny. After his machines were damaged by hand spinners in his native Oswaldtwistle, he moved to Nottingham and established a spinning mill in partnership with Thomas James. Ironically the jennies produced a weft yarn more suited to the cotton and linen weavers of Lancashire than to the Midlands knitting industry.

1769   Robert Arkwright patented a roller spinning frame, a modified and more successful variant of Lewis Paul's invention. He moved from Preston to Nottingham where his mechanically spun cotton warp threads were more suited than Hargreaves' for use on the stocking frame.

1771   Arkwright built his first water powered spinning mill at Cromford in Derbyshire. He devised a draw frame which coped with the intermediate process between carding and spinning, and produced even strands of yarn.

1773   Arkwright's yarns proved suitable for calico weaving as well as stocking knitting. Production expanded and cotton mills appeared in various parts of the country, but the largest number were in Lancashire.

1779   Samuel Crompton patented his 'mule'. This spinning machine produced a yarn which could be used for both warp and weft threads.

1785   Edmund Cartwright devised a power driven loom for weaving cotton materials, but it required considerable modification, and was not much used after his spinning and weaving factory at Doncaster closed in 1793.

COTTON PRINTING

1756 The Irish method of printing linen, calico or fustian with engraved relief metal plates was established at Merton near London. This allowed larger repeats and finer details to be printed. Additional colours were added by the traditional wood block method or painted onto the material.

1783 Thomas Bell patented a rotary printing machine which used engraved cylinders.

1785 By this date Bell had installed a machine which printed in six colours, near Preston, in close proximity to the Lancashire cotton weavers. It could do the work of 40 hand printers.

PRODUCTION OF WOOLLEN CLOTH

1784 Crompton's water powered spinning frames were adapted to spin worsted yarns. The industry began to shift away from East Anglia to Yorkshire where there was more water power.

KNITTING

1740 An addition to the knitting frame which could produce a line or rib down the stocking, was devised in Nottingham.

1758-59 Jedediah Strutt took out patents on additions to the stocking frame which produced a reverse loop for rib knitting.

c.**1775** The first warp knitting machine was invented, creating materials which could be treated in the same way as woven materials.

1777 William Betts improved this invention by developing a method whereby needles instead of sinkers moved to and fro, which created a knitting frame which could be worked by 'hand, horse or other power'.

Surviving costume

Many museums contain items of costume which date from this period, although it is unlikely that they will have many examples which are earlier than *c*.1740. What have survived are suits, dresses and accessories worn by the wealthier members of society. However, within these limits it is possible to see a wide range of examples made from British and imported materials. Not all of the museums listed below will have eighteenth-century examples on display, but they may be able to offer study facilities to serious students if given reasonable notice.

Museum of Costume, Bath

Museum and Art Gallery, Birmingham

Blaise Castle House, Bristol

Welsh Folk Museum, St Fagan's, Cardiff

Chertsey Museum

National Museum of Antiquities of Scotland, Edinburgh

Royal Scottish Museum, Edinburgh

Royal Albert Memorial Museum, Exeter

Churchill Gardens Museum, Hereford

Wygston's House Costume Museum, Leicester

Museum of London, London
Victoria and Albert Museum, London
Gallery of English Costume, Manchester
Museum of Costume and Textiles, Nottingham
Stranger's Hall, Norwich
Hartlebury Castle, Worcestershire County Museum
Museum and Art Gallery, Worthing
Castle Howard Costume Galleries, York
Castle Museum, York

1790-1849 Revolution and Reaction

The developments of the late eighteenth century had foreshadowed changes in attitudes towards men's and women's dress. Men's clothes were evolving into elegant but fairly sober garments which suited their more serious approach to business. Women's dress was lighter and freer, but was still wholly unsuited to any kind of serious pursuit. The French Revolution coincided with these changes and accelerated them, and gave the less restricting styles of female dress a strong push in the direction of unfettered freedom. This freedom disappeared at much the same time as the political status quo was restored in Europe, and for the remainder of this period women were exhorted to be ladylike, decorative but confined beings; the frivolity of their clothes affirmed their general acceptance of this role.

The improved transport system, the flow of goods from both home and foreign industries, the gradual shift from a rural to an urban based economy and continuing prosperity, led to the establishment of better and larger shops throughout the country. Changes in fashion were easier to follow as a wide variety of magazines and newspapers containing fashion plates and advertisements were introduced to a growing audience which included the newly rich manufacturers, industrialists and their families.

In the 1840s a new medium was introduced which could record people and their appearance with uncanny accuracy. Photography was an immediate success with people of all social classes, and sitters who could never have afforded to pay a visit to a portrait painter eagerly visited a photographer's studio. These early photographs are often quite a shock. Seeing people as they actually looked, without the flattering gloss of a painter's hand, can be immensely revealing. Some sitters were elegant and composed, many more were ill at ease, unflatteringly dressed in fashions that did not suit them, and crumpled in a way that no fashion plate would ever have suggested. Although these photographs contain none of the cruelty, and very little of the humour of the late eighteenth- and early nineteenth-century cartoons and caricatures, they have an immediacy which no recording medium had possessed before the invention of photography. In some intangible way they mark the division between the modern period and all that had preceded it.

Menswear

The period between 1790 and *c*.1810 was one of transition, with an uneasy mixture of country and formal Court styles. There were considerable variations in the length of coats and breeches, the size of collars and the decoration worn on them, before the styles settled down. Even the names of the garments were confusing, as familiar terms were used to describe unfamiliar styles.

DRESS COATS

This name was given to the tail coat of the 1780s when it was adopted for all full dress occasions except Court wear (*29*). From a fairly simple garment with three seams it changed and the body of the garment became longer and more fitted. Darts were introduced at the front waistline, and then became seams when the body and

A LONDON NUISANCE Pl.ª 1ª

Pafsing a MUD CART.

29   Engraving by R Dighton 1821. The wide stiffened collar of the dress coat reveals a good deal of the waistcoat and cravat; pantaloons are held taut by a strap under dress boots; a top hat completes a smart, daytime appearance

30 Fashion plate *c*.1833. The contrast between the restrained elegance of the men's full skirted frock coats, narrow trousers, dark top hats and plain gloves, and the exaggerated and extravagant appearance of the woman is very marked

front tails were cut separately. The darts introduced to give a better fit below the armhole had similarly become seams by about 1840. This provided a coat of six main pieces with five seams, a type of cut and construction which was used for all nineteenth-century men's coats which had fitted bodies and separate tails. For daywear the dress coat was single or double breasted, although it was often left open to show the waistcoat, shirt and cravat in the 1820s (*29*). From about 1820 until *c*.1840 coat collars were large and stiff; the coat fronts were padded, and the sleeves were fuller and gathered at the top of the armhole.

RIDING/MORNING COATS

This was a tail coat with sloping fronts, originally worn for riding and then adopted for other informal morning activities.

FROCK COATS

These coats were not related to the eighteenth-century frock coats. They first appeared in *c*.1815-16 and were a refinement of the great-coat. The body was fitted but the skirts were full, and at first it had a rather military aspect, with a standing collar and froggings. After various forms had been tried it eventually came to have a body constructed like the dress coat, but with knee-length skirts (*30*).

PALETOTS

The paletot was a loose-fitting coat which appeared in the 1830s and was worn for informal or sporting activities.

WAISTCOATS

These were waist-length, and could be either single or double breasted, with or without collars and revers according to individual taste or the current fashion. The standing collar disappeared completely after c.1830, and from about 1825 until the 1850s the front extended into a shallow point. In the 1830s and 1840s the fronts were padded to create a rounded, pouter-pigeon shape. Throughout the nineteenth century waistcoats were the most colourful and decorative items worn by men.

BREECHES AND PANTALOONS

Breeches became tighter in the 1790s, and were often cut on the cross grain from warp-knitted jersey materials to give a closer and smoother fit. They were worn until c.1830 for formal occasions, and until a later date by sportsmen and the elderly. Pantaloons, which were worn until the middle of the century, were similar to tightly fitting breeches, but longer. They extended to the mid calf until c.1817 and then lengthened to the ankle and were held under the foot by a strap (29).

Trousers appeared early in the century, but were barely distinguishable from pantaloons. A variety known as 'cossacks' were a wide trouser taken in at the waist and ankle with gathers or pleats.

OUTERWEAR

Greatcoats were worn very long, usually double breasted with a high collar and sometimes with a cape.

UNDERWEAR AND INFORMAL DRESS

Shirts were usually made of the finest and lightest weight of linen, sometimes with lawn or cambric fronts, collars and cuffs. The collar was very high as it had to turn over the broad cravats and stocks which were fashionable. A separate collar appeared in the 1820s. Drawers were often made of warp-knitted jersey to give a close fit under pantaloons. Dressing gowns were full length with fitted bodies and often made of rich materials. Country clothes and sports clothes were less fitted.

ACCESSORIES

Probably the most important accessories were the stocks and cravats which gave such a stiff-necked but imposing appearance to men's dress in this period. Stocks, pieces of shaped stiffening covered by a silky material and fastened at the back, were a military fashion which George IV popularised in the 1820s. They were less fashionable, although still worn, after 1840. Cravats were squares or triangles of lawn or muslin which were folded into a band and starched. Considerable skill went into their arrangement, and there were many different ways of tying them.

Other accessories were rather discreet: plain dark leather shoes or boots; plain leather gloves; tall wide brimmed hats or *chapeau bras* early in the century, replaced in the 1820s by high-crowned top hats (*29*).

Women's clothes

The 1790s were a transitional period when women experimented with a variety of softer styles derived from the *chemise de la reine* and the *robe à l'Anglaise*. The neo-classical styles which were adopted in France were influential throughout Europe, and the angular line dictated by the long, stiff corsets of the eighteenth century was replaced by a more rounded, womanly shape.

ROUND ROBES

These combined the soft gathered skirt of the *chemise de la reine* with the fitted bodice of the *robe à l'Anglaise* (*31*), but as the waistline rose the back seams were reduced to two, and these seams

31 Fashion plate, January 1795. Open robes of silk are worn over silk and muslin round robes; these transitional fashions were a mixture of simplicity of cut with elaborately decorative accessories

SHEPHERDS, I HAVE LOST MY WAIST!
HAVE YOU SEEN MY BODY?
SACRIFICED TO MODERN TASTE
I'M QUITE A HODDY DODDY!

London. Pub. by Will.ᵐ Holland, No 50, Ox...

ᵗNEWTON del a fecit

32 Cartoon by R Newton, November 1795. This drawing skilfully caricatures the unbalanced and fussy fashions which *31* had recommended to its public as the height of elegance

were set back and the sleeves set well into the bodice to form a narrow backed bodice (*33*). At the front the bodice was gathered at the neck and the waist, and worn with a separate or attached *fichu.* The skirt was unfitted, with gathered fullness at the front, and box pleats over a small pad at the centre back. The sleeves came in various lengths, but were always close-fitting.

As the French neo-classical fashions were copied at the turn of the century, all fullness was eliminated from the bodice, which fitted closely and was low cut. The skirt was gored or gathered slightly at the sides and back and had a long train. Sometimes tunic overskirts were worn over these slim, transparent dresses. Variations in the styles of bodice and sleeves were introduced in the early 1800s, and sometimes the bodice was cut on the cross grain for a better fit.

In the 1790s an open robe was often worn over the round robe (*32*), or over a petticoat. This style derived its fitted bodice from the *robe à l'Anglaise.* It could be open-fronted, or have a closed skirt or a tailed skirt set well to the sides of the bodice as an echo of the fashionable man's tail coat.

DRESSES

By the second decade of the nineteenth century the dress bodice had evolved into the two main forms which were worn by most women until the 1840s. One had a gathered bodice, cut on the straight grain of the material, with fullness evenly distributed around the neckline and all the gathers drawn towards the centre front (*30*); the second type had a fitted front cut on the cross grain with two darts running from the centre of each breast to the centre front. The backs of both bodices were of the same structure as the round robe, and were fastened by ties, small buttons or hooks and eyes. The armhole had returned to its natural position. The sleeves and bodice became more decorated, and as the skirt widened to form a rather stiffer triangle, the sleeves widened to balance this new line. The waistline gradually returned to its natural level, and by the mid 1820s the skirt was set into a slightly pointed waistband. These changes were gradual, and the padded hems, ankle-length skirts, fitted bodices and decorated full sleeves of the 1820s can be traced back, through contemporary fashion plates, to preceding years.

In the late 1820s when the sleeves were so wide that they needed special supports (*33*), the bodices were equally imposing, with wide necklines and pleated or draped fronts (*34*). These dresses had ankle-length skirts which were pleated into the waistband. By the 1830s the skirts were gathered and their extra fullness was held out over a padded roll or small bustle. Just as the width of the sleeves seemed to have reached absurd and impractical proportions (*30*), it quickly subsided in the mid 1830s, and a new style which was equally restricting, but more balanced, replaced it.

The dresses of the late 1830s and 1840s had a bodice which grew longer and more pointed at the front, with the side sections cut on the cross grain, but with a straight grain front. The front fullness was arranged into stitched pleats, and evening dress bodices had a low, horizontal neckline. All the seams of these dresses were boned, and tightly fitting sleeves were inserted into an off the shoulder armhole. The effect was more graceful than the extremes of the late 1820s and early 1830s (*35*), but it imposed severe limitations on body movements. Skirts became longer, sometimes with flounces round the hem, and the extra width was supported over stiffened petticoats. These dresses were usually laced at the back of the bodice.

OUTERWEAR

Apart from the usual array of capes and mantles which provided warmth and comfort for travelling, there were other, more elegant outer garments. From the early years of the century until the 1820s spencers and pelisses were worn over dresses. The former was a waist length jacket with a high collar and long sleeves; the latter was similar to the open robe, with a fitted bodice, long sleeves and a full length skirt which was worn open or partly buttoned. When the large sleeves became fashionable such elegant jackets or light coat-dresses were no longer suitable; they were replaced by capes with wide, hanging sleeves. In the late 1830s and 1840s various styles of loose or semi-fitted capes and mantles were worn over the fuller skirts and fitted bodices.

33 Underwear 1825-35. Sleeve puffs were an essential support for the wide sleeved dresses of the late 1820s and 1830s; all underwear was fairly plain, made of white linen or cotton

34 Day dress 1828-30. White muslin with ribbons; the complicated bodice decoration is a characteristic feature of late 1820s dresses; cashmere shawls were light enough not to flatten the sleeves

UNDERWEAR AND INFORMAL WEAR

Women began to wear pantaloons and drawers in the early years of the nineteenth century. The former were originally worn by young girls but were soon copied by older women, particularly when thin, semi-transparent materials became popular. Drawers were a French fashion and did not become generally acceptable until the late 1830s. They consisted of two loose leg coverings attached to a waistband.

A new type of corset appeared early in the century. It was a long underbodice fitted to the body curves by the addition of gussets which allowed for the rounded shape of bust and hips. It had a front busk and back bones and was laced at the back. More seams and bones were introduced as the waistline returned to its natural position.

Stiffened petticoats, made of crin (horsehair) were worn under the widening skirts of the late 1830s and 1840s.

35 Fashion plate 1848. Day dress and wedding dress with the graceful fitted bodices, narrow sleeves and full skirts of the 1840s; movement was restricted by the rigid corsets and off the shoulder armholes

ACCESSORIES

These were light and decorative to complement the light dress materials. They included fur and silk tippets and muffs (*31*), kashmir shawls and copies made in Paisley and Norwich; flat leather and satin pumps with ribbon ties; plain gloves; small reticules; fans. Headwear changed from full caps to swathed turbans, from small bonnets to wide brimmed hats (*30*).

English materials

The change in fashions benefited certain parts of the English textile industry, but adversely affected the rest. The demand for fine cottons and lightweight worsteds dealt a severe blow to the silk industry, and delayed modernisation of the heavy wool cloth industry.

WOOL

The greatest home and overseas demand was for light to medium weight wool cloth such as superfine, kerseymere or broadcloth. These materials were suitable for the fitted coats of the period (*29*). A mixed material suitable for summer cloths, with a cotton warp and worsted weft was introduced into England from America in 1825 and was well established by the late 1830s.

Breeches, pantaloons and trousers were usually made of a lighter weight material, possibly jerseyweave or merino wools. Only greatcoats and other types of outerwear needed heavy woollen cloths.

LINEN

The main centres of production were in the north of England, in Scotland and in Ireland where fine quality linen for underwear was manufactured.

COTTON

The demand for plain and printed cottons increased as women's clothes became lighter and more flowing from the 1790s onwards (*31*). The range of cotton materials, muslins, lawns, cambrics and gauzes, both plain and patterned, increased throughout this period. Even when silks reappeared as a fashionable material in the 1820s, cotton was still in demand for summer clothes. Because cotton was a cheap, easily laundered material it began to replace wool as the material which poorer people could afford to wear.

Nearly all cottons were produced in the Manchester area and in Scotland.

SILK

This industry was in gradual decline throughout the nineteenth century. The Spitalfields industry never successfully adapted itself to cope with the changing fashions, but silk ribbons were woven in Coventry from the late eighteenth century and were an important decoration on dresses and headwear. Macclesfield produced attractive dress silks and received considerable royal patronage, and there was also a steady demand for mixed silk and wool materials.

LACE

Although a knitted open weave ground for needlerun lace was produced in Nottingham as early as 1769, it was not until 1809 when machine made net was produced for the first time, that the English lace industry began to produce lace which was able to compete with foreign imports. The novelty and lightness of the new embroidered net laces was a strong threat to the established handmade laces of the East Midlands and Devonshire, and the earliest machine made lace factories were established in the East Midlands, around Nottingham. It was not until Queen Victoria commissioned handmade Honiton lace for her wedding dress and trousseau in 1840 that the balance between the two sections of the industry began to be redressed.

Foreign materials

SILK

The ban on silks from France was lifted in 1826, and although French silks had been used surreptitiously before this date, they soon regained the leading position in the English market. They had been adapted to meet the demand for crisp, lightweight silks in the 1820s, and the silk makers continued to adapt their industry to meet new fashions throughout the nineteenth century.

LACE

The finest handmade lace was imported from France and Belgium, and the quality of design and workmanship in those two countries also created a considerable demand for their machine made laces.

ACCESSORIES

The prohibition on foreign luxury goods, which was lifted in 1826, led to large imports of European gloves, shoes, fans and shawls. Some of these goods were cheaper than home produced ones, others were quite simply more elegant and better made. French gloves, for example, quickly became the most popular fashion gloves because they fitted well and were reasonably priced.

Makers and construction

Tailors concentrated more on the fit of men's clothes. English tailors with their long experience of working with wool cloth, and their ability to give clothes made from wool a very distinctive elegance, soon led the field in European tailoring. For the first time in many centuries foreigners actually wanted to order their clothes from English tailors.

The closely fitting styles caused tailors to recognise the inadequacies of their previous methods of making clothes. The invention of the tape measure, early in the century, enabled accurate calculations to be made about the relationship of the various measurements of the body. This new knowledge led to a flood of tailors' manuals regarding the geometrical rules which could be applied to the proportions of the body. Garments were still cut from patterns, but the pattern blocks were now based on one or other of these new systems, and then adapted for a customer.

Dressmakers were also finding ways of coping with the increasingly complicated and decorated styles which succeeded the simple round robe. This skill was appreciated by their customers, and acknowledged by contemporary writers. The author of the *Workwoman's Guide*, 1838, stated ' . . . it is strongly recommended to all those who can afford it, to have their dresses made by a mantua maker, as those which are cut at home seldom fit so comfortably or look so well as as when made by persons in constant practice.' Dressmakers could acquire sets of fashionable patterns by buying them from the firms which specialised in supplying 'models made up in paper'. Ready made garments, of the unfitted variety, were always available, and by the mid 1840s 'sewed muslin dresses' were being advertised.

Shops

Shopping habits did not change very quickly during this period. New shops opened in greater numbers outside London, but they tended to follow the traditional pattern of only stocking a certain, specialised range of goods. Shopping was still a leisurely activity.

In London the fashionable shopping areas moved further westwards (*36*), and elegant groups of new shops opened in Regent Street and in small arcades which were conveniently covered as a protection from the elements.

Visits to the nearest large town became easier as roads improved and more forms of public transport were introduced, but in the isolated parts of the country people still depended on regular visits from travelling salesmen.

Prices

1790 For a fine green coat faced with uncut velvet and with a scarlet collar, £3 8s

1790 For two buff kerseymere breeches and two kerseymere waist-coats, £4 10s

1792 For a chintz gown (from a Scotchman), £2 10s

1797 For a black coat of secondhand cloth, £2 5s

1803 For a black silk sarsnet dress, £5 6s

1806 For a pair of cotton drawers (women's), 3s 9d

1808 For a best beaver and patent silk hat, £1 2s

1819 For a superfine black cloth dress coat, £7 3s 6d

1819 For a superfine cloth dress waistcoat, £1 10s

1828 For a rich figured India silk morning gown, £8 8s

Technical developments

PRODUCTION OF COTTON

1825 Richard Roberts invented an automatic mule which speeded up the spinning of yarn.

1835 Over 100 000 power looms were weaving cotton materials.

COTTON PRINTING

*c.*1810 From this time onwards English and European chemists were experimenting with new chemical resists and discharges, and with a new range of mineral based colours.

1834 A dye derived from coal tar, called kyanol, was introduced. This was part of a long process of experimentation which resulted in improved, fast, brilliantly coloured synthetic dyes.

PRODUCTION OF LINEN

1790 A patent was taken out by Matthew Murray on flax processing machinery.

1814-25 Experiments took place with the wet spinning of flax using the ideas of Philippe de Girard and James Kay.

1839 J Schofield and E Leach took out a patent on a power driven loom suitable for linen.

PRODUCTION OF WOOLLEN CLOTH

1792 Edmund Cartwright developed a wool combing machine for worsteds.

1830-40   Power looms were adapted for the weaving of worsted yarn.

38   Power loom weaving from *The History of Cotton Manufacture,* **1835. Power loom weaving was the reason for the increased output and cheapness of cotton goods in the nineteenth century; many women worked in factories wearing simple, practical clothes made of cotton**

KNITTING

1791   William Dawson's invention of a notched wheel acted as a selecting medium for the production of patterns.

1816   M I Brunel took out a patent on a circular knitting machine, but at first little use was made of this invention.

1847   M Townsend added a mechanism to Brunel's machine which produced rib knitted material of an ideal elasticity for stockings.

MACHINE MADE LACE

1809   John Heathcoat patented his bobbin net machine which exactly reproduced the thread movements of handmade lace.

Surviving costume

All of the museums listed at the end of the previous chapter will certainly contain some complete and a quantity of incomplete items and accessories from the period 1790-1849. However, from this time onwards far fewer examples of menswear survive, and women's dress of the 1820s and 1830s is also rather rare. Any student wanting to work with items from this period would be well advised to find out what might be available for study before selecting a topic. Several museums have published catalogues of their early nineteenth-century collections which can prove most helpful, and attempts to read one or more of these would be a useful preparation for a study visit to see local examples. A list of these catalogues is given in the bibliography.

In addition to the museums listed in the previous chapter there are other collections which contain some surviving items from this date, namely:

The Bowes Museum, Barnard Castle, Co.Durham

Cecil Higgins Art Gallery Bedford, (lace)

The Hollytrees, Colchester

Herbert Museum and Art Gallery, Coventry

Museum and Art Gallery, Glasgow

Museum and Art Gallery, Hitchin

Kirkstall Abbey House, Leeds

Lotherton Hall, Leeds

City Museum and Art Gallery, Liverpool

Museum and Art Gallery Luton, (especially lace and straw hats)

Laing Museum and Art Gallery, Newcastle

Museum and Art Gallery Paisley, (shawls)

Harris Museum and Art Gallery, Preston

Salisbury and South Wiltshire Museum, Salisbury

1850-1900 Victorian Confidence

In the second half of the nineteenth century speed and output in the textile manufacturing industries increased. Ready to wear clothing was being mass produced, and there was more publicity for all aspects of men's and women's fashions in magazines and newspapers. The population of Great Britain was growing quickly, and the change from a rural based to an urban based economy became more marked. Although there were still considerable social divisions, many newly rich merchants and manufacturers and their families were able to afford expensive and luxurious goods. Consequently, the range of goods and the number of shops enlarged to meet the growing demand.

The mechanisation of the clothing and footwear trades in the wake of the invention of the sewing machine reduced the price of ready to wear goods, and enabled the majority of the population to afford sturdy, well made garments. Charles Booth, who spent much of his life helping the working classes, said of an average working man and his family that '. . . clothes necessary for comfort are usually good and suitable . . . they wear well . . .[and] as a rule, none of the clothes are secondhand.'

The sober and sensible appearance of men's clothes contrasted very sharply with the brightly coloured, highly decorated and rather substantial elegance of women's clothes (*colour plate 3, facing page 25*). Both sexes, but more particularly women, looked like the sturdily upholstered furniture which could be seen in Victorian homes, well padded, richly covered and extravagantly trimmed. This human upholstery was very well made. English tailoring was considered the finest in Europe, but the emergence of the new breed of imaginative designer/dressmaker, whose judgment in the area of women's fashions was considered superior to the customer's, took place in France. Ironically the first of these great designers was an Englishman, Charles Worth, who received his training in London shops, but went to Paris to perfect his craft.

The constantly changing fashions and the restrictions that they imposed did not suit everyone, and those individuals who wanted more comfortable, and less restricting clothing, played an important part in the dress reform and aesthetic dress movements of the second half of the nineteenth century. These movements fall outside the mainstream of fashion history, and, at first, they received more ridicule than support, but they contain the germ of the twentieth-century desire for elegance combined with unrestricted comfort.

Menswear

By the second half of the nineteenth century it is possible to identify, in their early form, all the items of men's clothing which can be found in a present day man's wardrobe.

ye GORGEOUS YOUNG SWELLS!—

39 The 'gorgeous young swells' (1878)
are wearing elegantly cut high buttoned
frock coats, high starched collars and
cravats; patterned trousers were rarely
acceptable with frock coats until later

DRESS/MORNING COATS

The dress coat was correct formal wear for day and evening functions
in the 1850s, but by the 1860s it was usually worn only in the
evening. Its basic shape hardly ever changed, and only small details
marked the passage of time. In the 1850s it was replaced by its close

relative, the frock coat, for formal daytime wear. This became a slimmer skirted, slightly looser fitting garment in the 1860s, and continued to be worn well into the twentieth century (*39*).

However, by 1880 it too had been overtaken by another style of coat, the 'morning coat', a tail coat with sloping front edges which had evolved from the riding coat.

THREE PIECE SUITS

This was an established style of dress by the late 1860s (*40*), and was popular for informal daytime wear. It had developed quite gradually, firstly with the matching of waistcoats with trousers in the 1850s, and then with the addition of the 'lounge jacket', which was a rather more fitted version of the paletot of the 1830s. These three-piece suits were usually made of tweed or checked or plaid material.

40 Charles Dickens and his daughters, photograph *c*.1863. Dickens is wearing a three-piece suit with an informal turned down collar and neck-tie; his daughters are dressed in summer cottons over moderately full crinolines

JACKETS

The popularity of the lounge jacket led to allied styles, namely the smoking jacket, the 'dress lounge' and the Norfolk jacket. The first was always an informal garment, but the second, which appeared as an informal evening jacket in 1888, soon developed into the dinner jacket of the mid to late 1890s. The third type of jacket was a sporting version, with box pleats at the back and front and a belt.

WAISTCOATS

These were always black or white for formal occasions. Fancy waist-coats were still worn in the 1850s and 1860s, but by the late 1870s all waistcoats were hidden by high buttoned coats (*39*). There was a brief revival of patterned waistcoats in the 1890s.

TROUSERS

The shape of trousers changed from the 'peg tops' of the late 1850s to a straighter line in the 1860s. Although braid on the outside leg was a feature of dress trousers, a centre crease did not appear until the 1890s.

OUTERWEAR

Several warm and comfortable coats appeared. Two of the most popular were the Inverness cape, which was a loose overcoat with an arm length cape (*colour plate 3, facing page 25*); and the Ulster, which was a long, belted coat with a detachable hood. A smart overcoat for more formal wear was the Chesterfield which was narrower in cut than the others, and rather shorter. In the evening black capes were worn over dress clothes.

UNDERWEAR AND INFORMAL DRESS

Nineteenth-century shirts had a yoke, and a longer tail at the back than the front. They usually buttoned at the centre front, and dress shirts had a stiffened front panel. Collars were almost invariably detachable, and although unstarched, turn-down collars were acceptable for informal wear (*40*), it was more usual for men to wear upright starched collars. These were fairly narrow until the 1890s when they started to heighten until they reached a height of 75 mm (3 in.) by 1896. From the early 1860s until the late 1880s coats buttoned up high to the neck, so little could be seen of the cravat. Cravats came in several varieties but were most prominent in the 1890s.

During this period there were additions to basic underclothing in the form of Dr Jaeger's pure wool combinations or vests and under-pants. He introduced these for hygienic reasons, but they became popular because they provided extra warmth.

Men still wore nightshirts in bed, and covered them with dressing gowns of thick padded and quilted materials before dressing.

ACCESSORIES

As the general trend was towards uniformity in dress for town wear, the accessories which were worn were similarly rather characterless and sombre in appearance. Plain dark top hats, boots, shoes and gloves were usual, although in the country there was a certain amount of choice in colour and style.

Women's clothes

DRESSES

The dresses of the 1850s were fairly graceful, with the bust and waist in their natural places, emphasised by a fitted bodice and a modestly full skirt (*41*). As the skirt grew fuller it had to be supported over a cage or crinoline (*42*), and in the 1860s, as the waistline rose, the skirt became gored, and the line of the dress flattened at the front and extended into a train at the back. The absurd size and shape of the crinoline excited a good deal of critical comment, and many cartoons (*43*), but in 1867 it began to subside, and the surplus material was taken back and arranged over a bustle.

41 *right:* Unknown woman, photograph *c* 1862. The dress and hat are similar to those worn by one of Dickens' daughters (*40*), but this sitter wears a wider crinoline and is more self conscious about her appearance

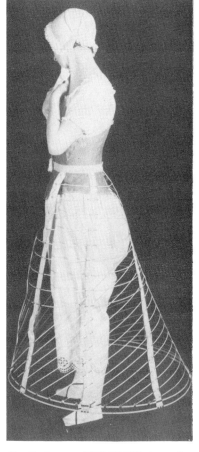

42 Underwear 1860-70. This type of underwear, consisting of a cage crinoline worn over a short sleeved chemise, drawers and a scarlet cotton corset, with the addition of one or two petticoats, would have been worn under the dresses in *40* and *41*

Between the late 1860s and the early 1880s the line became slimmer and longer bodied at the front of the dress, and the waistline returned to its natural place. The back fullness of the skirt was arranged in flounces, puffs and draperies over the bustle. The narrow lines of these dresses (*44*) required such excellent workmanship from dressmakers, and such slim, elegant figures, that disguise for the lack of one or both was provided in the form of front draperies and lots of trimmings (*45*).

43 Cartoon 1859. The crinoline excited a good deal of ridicule because of its impracticality; in the 1860s girls working in a Staffordshire china factory were fined £200 in one year for the breakages caused by their crinolines

In the 1880s the severity of line was alleviated by draped bodices and a bustle which extended to form a plateau at the back of the skirt, creating one of the ugliest silhouettes ever seen in women's fashions. As the bustle, like the crinoline before it, collapsed once it had reached a size that made further expansion impossible, the emphasis shifted to a more womanly line of a full, rounded bust, tiny waist and rounded hips (49). Skirts began to widen and were balanced by fuller sleeves, although by c.1895 it was the very full sleeves that dominated the dress. In the last few years of the century the sleeves grew tighter and the bodices developed a soft, pouched fullness which overhung the waistband (50).

Nearly all dresses were made in two pieces, although in the 1880s the narrow line sometimes dictated a one-piece dress. In the 1860s dresses with two bodices, a daytime one and an evening one, became popular, and this economical fashion continued into the 1870s. From about 1863 the princess line dress, cut without a waist seam, became popular, and looked forward to the narrower dresses of the late 1870s and 1880s. The necklines of day dresses were usually fairly modest, and in the 1880s high collars appeared and remained in fashion until the end of the century (49). They were matched by long sleeves or three-quarter length sleeves worn over cotton under-sleeves. Evening dresses were usually low cut with short sleeves, although narrow straps began to replace sleeves in the late 1880s.

44   Fashion plate from *The Queen*
1877. The narrow lines of 1870s dresses
were broken up with considerable
decoration; although many of these
dresses were machine stitched, nearly all
the decoration was applied by hand

BLOUSES AND SKIRTS

In the 1860s blouses began to be worn with skirts for informal
occasions. In the 1880s blouses were joined by 'habit shirts', loose
fitting blouses which originated as thin undershirts for dresses or
riding habits (*50*).

Separate skirts were made in the same way as dress skirts, but
were often of darker and more hard wearing materials.

SUITS

Women had worn loose-fitting jackets with matching skirts from the
late 1850s, but the crisply tailored jacket suits of the 1880s were
derived from riding habits, and similarly were often the work of
tailors rather than dressmakers.

OUTERWEAR

Tailors were making coats and jackets for women from *c*.1850
onwards, but the majority of women preferred capes and mantles
until the 1870s. In the 1870s and 1880s the styles of dresses led to
the introduction of the dolman, a shaped three-quarter length cape
or coat which could accommodate a bustle. Fur jackets made of seal-
skin and beaver appeared in the 1870s and retained their popularity
for the rest of the century. In the 1890s shaped capes, of various
lengths, were worn over the full sleeved dresses.

45 Day dress 1878. Grey silk dress trimmed with pillow lace; a Princess line dress with a 'fish-tail' train

UNDERWEAR AND INFORMAL DRESS

The corset was the most important undergarment, and its changing shape and length can be determined by closely studying the fashions worn over it. Corsets were always heavily boned and often had a firm centre busk bone. They were mass produced once it was realised that the sewing machine could be used to stitch them. Other important items of underwear were the crinolines and bustles which supported the shape of the skirt. These were lightweight structures made from cane, steel or crin (*42*).

Other types of underwear which were worn included chemises and drawers, camisole tops and combination camisoles and drawers, and corset covers. Petticoats varied from substantial red flannel to the lightest silk taffetas. Corsets, crinolines and bustles were often coloured, but other underwear was usually white with coloured ribbon decoration. Nightdresses were also white, but trimmed with lace or embroidery. Dressing gowns were made of coloured and patterned materials.

One important item of informal dress, closely related to the dressing gown, was the tea-gown. This was an unboned, loose-fitting dress which first appeared in the 1870s to allow women to relax in an elegant but uncorseted dress. Surviving examples are usually very pretty, made from soft, lightweight materials, with

46 Fashion plate from *The Queen,* 1884. The exaggerated bustles of these dresses created an unflattering silhouette which emphasised a small waist and rounded bust but completely distorted the hips

pleats, ruching and lace decoration. By the end of the century they were considered formal enough for receiving visitors in.

ACCESSORIES

Women's accessories were so pretty and so varied that it is impossible to do justice to them in a short description. All types of accessory changed as frequently as fashion changed, but they were always complementary to the prevailing style whether it was formally tailored or elaborately pretty.

English materials

WOOL

Heavy wool materials were less popular than worsteds until the late 1850s when the industry adapted itself to meet the demand for heavier weight cloth for country and sporting clothes for men. The more formal menswear was made from firm light and medium weight cloth with a smooth finish, such as superfine, broadcloth and kersey-mere. Flannel was first used for men's suits in the 1890s.

Women's clothes used a wider variety of woollen cloth than ever before ranging from lightweight wools such as cashmere and merino in the 1850s and 1860s to serges and tweeds in the 1870s and 1880s and returning to the lighter worsteds, cashmeres and mohairs in the 1890s.

47 Dress and bonnet 1885-86. Crimson velvet and satin with bead trimming; this example is less tightly fitting at the skirt front and looks less unbalanced than those depicted in fashion plates

LINEN

There was an active linen industry in Ireland which produced fine grade material for underclothes and summer wear.

COTTON

There was a positive flood of cheap printed cotton materials, and other more expensive cottons. Piqués and muslins were used for women's summer dresses, and imitations of silks, like sateen, plush and velveteen gained in popularity.

SILK

Macclesfield silks were fairly popular, and there was constant demand for mixed silk and wool and silk and cotton materials.

LACE

Machine made lace was widely used as a trimming and for accessories like shawls (41), caps and veils. The designs often copied more expensive foreign laces, but at a fraction of the cost. Handmade lace

48 Bustle 1884. White cotton with curved steels; bustles came in various sizes and forms; some dresses had a built-in bustle

was popular for wedding and trousseau garments, but it was very expensive.

Foreign materials

WOOL

The major imports were specialist wool yarns which were woven into fashionable materials like cashmere, mohair or merino cloths.

SILK

The finest dress weight silks were imported from France. Lightweight, unstiffened silks were imported from the Far East, and were particularly popular with women who wore 'aesthetic' dress.

LACE

Handmade and machine made lace was imported from France, Belgium and certain other countries. Chantilly lace was particularly fashionable, and there were both expensive handmade and cheaper machine made types.

TRIMMINGS AND ACCESSORIES

Many of these were imported, as they were either less expensive or

49   Fashion plate from *The Queen*
1890. Dresses of the early 1890s had a
restrained elegance with little obvious
distortion of the body

of better quality than their English counterparts. French fans, gloves
and shoes were widely admired.

Makers and construction

English tailoring was admired for its perfection of cut and fit. All
men's clothes were very well finished, and full linings became the
norm rather than the exception. All large cities and many towns had
a number of tailor's shops where advice about materials, current
styles and alterations could be sought. Mass production tailoring was
an area of considerable growth, and ready to wear men's clothes,
although less well fitting and made from cheaper materials, were
based on the same systems of mathematical tailoring which were
applied to bespoke customers.

Women's clothes were made by dressmakers, tailors and at home.
Dressmakers, in their own workrooms or in the workrooms of a large
shop, worked from the paper patterns which were generally available
to professional dressmakers. In the 1850s women's magazines started
to publish patterns for bodices, mantles and underwear which could
be made by home dressmakers. There were also various useful
handbooks on dressmaking. For the less skilful there were partly
made dresses, usually finished skirts with a length of material which
could be made into a bodice. Later in the century fully made up
garments could be bought from many shops.

Home dressmaking and professional dressmaking was assisted by
the introduction of the sewing machine. Until the end of the century

the majority of clothes were hand finished, but machines coped speedily with seams and darts. Professionally made dresses were very well put together with lined bodices skilfully boned, and skirts were lined if the material was heavy or rough.

Shops

By the second half of the nineteenth century all cities, large towns and many villages had shops or a shop where materials, trimmings and articles of clothing could be purchased. There were many specialist shops in the larger cities and towns which carried a wide range of goods at various prices, and even the poorest members of society could 'window shop' for ideas which might cheaply renovate an outmoded garment. Shop windows were full of goods, and attracted custom with their ' . . . numberless lace trifles, gaudy ribbons, satins, delicate frills and confections and head-dresses.' This description, given by Lady Violet Greville in the 1880s, has a disapproving ring to it, but increased industrialisation and mass production had brought many more of these goods within the range of a wider cross section of society.

Shops catered for a customer's every need, from Christmas clothing parcels for employers to give to their female servants, to £5 'travelling portmanteaux' for gentlemen who had to undertake an unexpected journey. This anticipation of the customer's every need was the hallmark of a successful shop.

The major development in this period was the departmental shop in which a customer could buy everything under one roof. The earliest example was William Whiteley's shop in Westbourne Grove in London. He opened in 1863 selling ribbons, lace and fancy goods, and within five years had expanded to include silks, linens, mantles, drapery, millinery, ladies' outfitting, furs, umbrellas and artificial flowers. In the 1870s he added groceries, meat, ironmongery, books, a house agency, outside catering, hairdressing, dry cleaning and a laundry service. By 1878 *Whiteley's Diary and Almanac* had announced a delivery service for London and the suburbs, and goods could be dispatched by train to the provinces.

This new sort of shop frightened and angered small businessmen, but Whiteley's lead was quickly followed throughout London, and in provincial cities and towns. Such large shops attracted customers from all over London, and from as far away as Bath or Cambridge (this was made possible by the speed and frequency of railway services), and many of these departmental shops added restaurants and cloakrooms for their customers' benefit.

At the other end of the spectrum were the Penny Bazaars, started in Manchester by Michael Marks in the 1890s. They were similar to market stalls, with open displays, goods from a wide variety of trades, and the cheapness made possible by self selection and a fast turnover. There were also multiple shops, and by the end of the century it was possible to buy Freeman, Hardy and Willis boots and shoes in over 100 branches throughout the country.

Although it is possible, with hindsight, to see these developments as precursors of twentieth-century methods of shopping, there was still plenty of custom for the smaller shops. Many people preferred smaller shops for all sorts of reasons, including their prices. Departmental shops were not always the cheapest shops, as Mrs M V Hughes indicates in her book, *A London Home in the Nineties*: 'Bessie . . .

advised me to get everything at Whiteley's. "You've only got to walk into the shop, order what you want in the different departments, and you find everything delivered at your door." She was right, but I soon found that this easy way of buying had to be paid for by too high prices, so I determined to explore the neighbourhood, buy what I wanted, and bring it home myself.'

Prices

1855 For six pairs of morning and one pair of evening trousers, £9

1855 For four morning and one evening waistcoat, £4

1862 For a lace and muslin double skirt dress, from 15s 9d

1862 For a machine made Brussels lace square, from 1gn

1874 For a Honiton lace bridal veil, from 5gns to 50gns

1886 For an unmade muslin embroidered dress (sale price) 19s 6d — 70s

1887 For a cashmere shawl, from £30 — £500

1888 For a dressing gown, 1gn

1890 For a day suit, 5gns

1894 For a classical Grecian tea-gown of French crepon, £4 4s

Technical developments

The most important development was the invention of the sewing machine, which was a crucial factor in the move towards the mass production of clothing. A variety of European and American inventors contributed to its production, but the real breakthrough was made by Isaac Singer who patented his lockstitch machine in 1850. It was sold in America and Europe from the late 1850s onwards, and although other firms produced machines, Singer was the most successful in the field of both domestic and industrial machines.

PRODUCTION OF WOOLLEN CLOTH

1860-70 A new combing machine was introduced which successfully speeded up this process.

1887 Mr Noble's combing device was introduced into the woollen mills leading to the production of surplus yarn which was exported to Europe and America.

PRODUCTION OF COTTON

1850-60 The American ring spinning frame began to replace the mule.

COTTON PRINTING

1856 Fast dyes for printing all types of material, including cotton, were introduced. They were called aniline dyes and were developed from coal tar. Although different treatments were needed for different materials they were an immediate success.

1884 The first cotton dye not to need a mordant, azo dye, was discovered.

SYNTHETIC MATERIALS

1892 The first artificial silk was spun from chemically treated wood pulp. This invention was not used commercially until the twentieth century.

Surviving costume

All museums which collect costume will have some items which date from the second half of the nineteenth century. The majority of examples will be women's clothes or accessories, although enough items of menswear survive for comparisons to be made between the divergent styles of the two sexes. In some museums there may be a few items of working or occupational dress.

From the late 1860s dressmakers usually placed labels in the clothes they made, so it is possible to assess the differences, if any, between the fashions worn in a particular part of the country, and the fashions which were shown in the contemporary magazines.

Apart from the many museums listed on pages 61 and 75 there will be other museums which may be able to offer study facilities in their galleries or reserve collections to serious students. These museums can be identified in the *ABC Guide to Museums and Galleries* (see bibliography).

50 Queen Victoria and her family at Osborne, photograph 1898. The younger girls are wearing skirts and blouses with the fashionable pouched front bodice; the older women favour tailored suits; the Duke of York is wearing a light-weight summer suit

Projects in Costume History

This section is intended for students who have to select a topic of their own, without guidance from an examination syllabus. These suggestions provide only a small selection of general and specialised topics which can be attempted without straying outside the mainstream of the history of fashion.

General topics

applicable to all periods

1 Select a period of between 20 and 40 years, and trace the main factors which influenced men's or women's costume within that period, eg the availability of materials, methods of tailoring, foreign influences, prices.

2 Select a particular decade and discuss all the items of clothing and accessories which a fashionable man or woman might need for daywear, or evening wear, or both. This information can be assembled in layers, eg underwear, suits and dresses, outerwear, accessories.

3 Assemble a series of illustrations from a period of 20 to 30 years and discuss what is known about the garments which are depicted, their construction, the materials used, their cost and availability.

4 Imagine that at any date in the past someone wanted to buy a new suit or dress. How did they go about realising this wish, how many processes were involved, and how much might they pay?

5 Discuss any particular advantages or disadvantages in wearing the fashions of a period of your choice. Consider comfort, warmth, restricted movement, ease of laundering, legality of certain materials.

6 Choose a play or novel that you admire and discuss the type of clothes three or four of the main characters might have worn at the date at which it was written. Consider the financial and social status of the characters, their age, their proximity to a major shopping centre, whether they are described as having good or bad taste in clothing.

Possible writers: Shakespeare, Congreve, Goldsmith, Sheridan, Jane Austen, Dickens, George Eliot, Wilkie Collins, Oscar Wilde.

7 Choose a period during which fashions of a fairly extreme nature were replaced by new styles. How quickly did the change occur and in what ways did the new styles differ from the old?

8 'The history of women's costume is really the history of their underclothes.' Discuss this statement in a period of your choice.

Specialised topics

applicable in certain parts of the country

These projects should not be attempted unless it is possible to make arrangements to discuss their feasibility with a local librarian, archivist or museum curator.

1 Consider the contribution that a local textile or fashion industry has made to the history of costume, and indicate how it prospered or declined as fashions changed.
Possible industries: wool in Yorkshire and East Anglia, cotton in Lancashire, knitting in the East Midlands, lacemaking in Devonshire or the East Midlands.

2 Make a detailed study of a small group of costumes on display, or in the reserve collection of a local museum. Explain how they are constructed and sewn and in what ways they changed over a short period of 10 or 20 years.

according to period

1 Contrast the clothes of the period 1500-1520 with those of 1580-1600. What major changes had taken place and were any new garments introduced?

2 The Puritans criticised the fashions of the period *c*.1610-1640 for their richness and frivolity. How did their clothes differ from those that they criticised?

3 Discuss the important changes which occurred in men's and women's clothing in the 1660s and 1670s, and consider why these changes happened.

4 'Eighteenth-century dress was both elegant and practical.' Discuss this statement with regard to the period 1720-1750 or 1760-1790.

5 'Men's clothes changed for the better, women's for the worse between 1820 and 1850.' Discuss this statement, and consider why the clothes of the two sexes were so different in terms of colour, cut, comfort and practicality.

6 Photography added an extra dimension to the study of nineteenth-century costume. Consider what it tells us about clothes and their wearers that other types of illustration cannot.

7 Why were the dress reform movements of the second half of the nineteenth-century necessary, and were they successful?

8 Consider the impact made on women's clothing by the sewing machine, ready made clothes and the departmental shop.

Glossary

Unusual or obsolete words which have been defined in the main text are not included in this glossary.

Baize A plain weave wool cloth

Birdseye tiffany A thin spotted silk

Broadcloth Pre 1800, a fine plain weave wool cloth Post 1800, a twilled wool cloth made from merino yarn with a dress finish

Budge Lambskin

Casaque A loose-fitting coat

Cashmere A fine twilled worsted, originally imported from Kashmir

Cassocke A loose coat

Cutwork Lace made from cut and drawn linen threads, embroidered with buttonhole stitches

Dymitie A twill weave fustian

Holmes fustian A type of fustian originally imported from Ulm in Germany

Kersey A coarse wool cloth, one of the Yorkshire narrow cloths in the eighteenth century

Kerseymere A fine twilled wool cloth

Lustring A fine, lustrous silk taffeta

Mantle A long cloak or cape

Merino A thin twilled woollen cloth originally made of Spanish merino sheep's wool

Pinking A decorative pattern of small holes or slits

Plush A shaggy piled cotton velvet

Reticule A lady's handbag of circular or lozenge shape

Sarsnet A thin plain or twilled silk

Sateen A cotton material with a shiny satin surface

Serge A loosely woven twilled material with a worsted warp and wool weft

Slashing An arrangement of decorative slits to reveal or display the garment beneath

Superfine Pre 1800, a broadcloth made of Spanish merino wool Post 1800, a broadcloth of merino yarn with a dress finish

Tawny A wool cloth usually of a brownish yellow colour

Tippet A short shoulder cape

Vermilion A cotton cloth dyed scarlet

Worsted A cloth made from fine, smooth long wool yarn, lighter than wool cloth

Bibliography

All of the books listed below have been published or reprinted during the last 20 years and, consequently, are still easily available. It is unlikely that all libraries with lending and reference sections will carry the full range, but they will order them for readers through the national inter-library loan service.

Source books, bibliographies and dictionaries

Anthony P and Arnold J, *Costume, A General Bibliography*, Costume Society 1977
Arnold J, *Handbook of Costume*, Macmillan 1974
Costume Society Journal, Costume Society, annually since 1965
Cunnington C W and P and Beard C, *A Dictionary of English Costume*, A and C Black reprinted 1976
Museums and Art Galleries in Great Britain and Ireland, Index, annually
Reader's Guide to Costume, Publication No.126, Library Association

General costume history

Boucher F, *A History of Costume in the West*, Thames and Hudson 1967
Bradfield N, *Costume in Detail*, Harrap 1968
Laver J, *A Concise History of Costume*, Thames and Hudson 1969
Moore D L, *Fashion through Fashion Plates 1770-1970*, Ward Lock 1971
Squire G, *Dress, Art and Society*, Studio Vista 1974

Sixteenth-century costume

Cunnington C W and P, *Handbook of English Costume in the Sixteenth Century*, Faber and Faber 1970 (revised edition)

Seventeenth-century costume

Cunnington C W and P, *Handbook of English Costume in the Seventeenth Century* Faber and Faber, third edition 1972

Eighteen-century costume

Buck A, *Dress in Eighteenth Century England*, Batsford 1979
Cunnington C W and P, *Handbook of English Costume in the Eighteenth Century* Faber and Faber, third edition 1966

Nineteenth-century costume

Buck A, *Victorian Costume and Costume Accessories*, Herbert Jenkins 1961
Cunnington C W and P, *Handbook of English Costume in the Nineteenth Century* Faber and Faber, reprinted 1973
Gernsheim A, *Fashion and Reality,* Faber and Faber 1963
Gibbs-Smith C H, *The Fashionable Lady in the Nineteenth Century*, HMSO 1960
Newton S M, *Health, Art and Reason*, John Murray 1974
Walkley C and Foster V, *Crinolines and Crimping Irons*, Peter Owen 1978

Menswear

Byrde P, *The Male Image*, Batsford 1979
Waugh N, *The Cut of Men's Clothes 1600-1900*, Faber 1964

Women's clothing

Ewing E, *Dress and Undress*, Batsford 1978
Waugh N, *Corsets and Crinolines*, Batsford, reprinted 1972
Waugh N, *The Cut of Women's Clothes 1600-1930*, Faber and Faber 1968

Makers and construction

Arnold J, *Patterns of Fashion, Part 1 1660-1860 Part 2 1860-1940*, Macmillan 1972

Shops

Adburgham A, *Shops and Shopping*, George Allen and Unwin 1964
Adburgham A, *Shopping in Style*, Thames and Hudson 1979
Harrison M, *People and Shopping*, Ernest Benn 1975

Materials and Techniques

Clabburn P, *The Needleworker's Dictionary,* Macmillan 1976
Digby G W, *Elizabethan Embroidery*, Faber and Faber 1963
Hughes T, *English Domestic Needlework*, Abbey Fine Arts n.d.

Robinson S, *History of Printed Textiles*, Studio Vista 1969

Thornton P, *Baroque and Rococo Silks*, Faber 1965

Wardle P, *Victorian Lace*, Herbert Jenkins 1968

Technical developments

English W, *The Textile Industry*, Longmans 1969

Gilbert K R, *Sewing Machines,* HMSO 1970

Gilbert K R, *Textile Machinery*, HMSO

Chambers Encyclopaedia, Encyclopaedia Britannica for articles on cotton, linen, silk, wool etc.

Surviving costume

All the museum catalogues listed below contain information about surviving items of costume. Many of these catalogues can be ordered from the museum concerned; a few are out of print, but may possibly be found in public libraries. Details of other museum booklets, leaflets and illustrations which may be of interest to the student, can be found in the first publication listed below.

A Guide to Costume and Textile Publications from Museums in Great Britain, Group for Costume and Textile Staff, 1980

BRISTOL MUSEUM AND ART GALLERY. Bennett H and Witt C, *Eighteenth-Century Women's Costume at Blaise Castle House*

CHERTSEY MUSEUM. Rowley C, *Costume in Chertsey Museum 1700-1800*

HULL MUSEUM. Crowther A, *Madame Clapham the Celebrated Dressmaker*

MUSEUM OF LONDON. Halls Z, *Men's Costume 1580-1750, 1750-1800; Women's Costume 1600-1750, 1750-1800*

MANCHESTER CITY ART GALLERIES. Buck A, *Women's Costume – A Brief View, The Eighteenth-Century, 1800-1835, 1835-1870, 1870-1900. 1870-1900.*

NORTHAMPTON MUSEUM. Swann J, *A History of Shoe Fashions*

NORWICH CASTLE MUSEUM. Clabburn P, *Norwich Shawls*

NOTTINGHAM MUSEUM AND ART GALLERY. Halls Z, *Machine Made Lace in Nottingham in the Eighteenth and Nineteenth Centuries*

HARRIS MUSEUM AND ART GALLERY, PRESTON. *Preston and Cotton; Images of Fashion – Fashion Plates 1770-1900*

WORCESTERSHIRE COUNTY MUSEUM. Bullard D, *Catalogue of the Costume Collection Part I 1645-1790, Part II 1800-1830*

WORTHING MUSEUM. Bullard D, *Catalogue of the Costume Collection Part I Eighteenth Century, Part II 1800-1830*

Index

The numerals in *italics* refer to the illustration numbers. (m) = male; (f) = female